W9-DEE-620

AN
ENCYCLOPEDIA
OF
CHAIRS

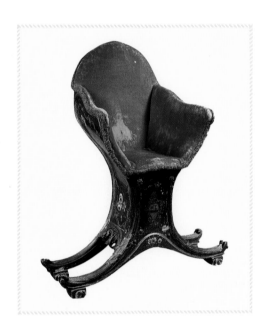

A N
ENCYCLOPEDIA
OF
CHAIRS

SIMON YATES

THE WELLFLEET PRESS

WELLFLEET

A QUINTET BOOK

Published by Wellfleet Press
110 Enterprise Avenue,
Secaucus, New Jersey 07094

Copyright © 1988 Quintet Publishing Limited.
All rights reserved. No part of this publication may
be reproduced, stored in a retrieval system or
transmitted in any form or by any means,
electronic, mechanical, photocopying, recording or
otherwise, without the permission of the copyright
holder.

ISBN 1-55521-268-9

This book was designed and produced by
Quintet Publishing Limited
6 Blundell Street
London N7 9BH

Art Director: Peter Bridgewater
Designer: James Lawrence
Editor: Caroline Beattie
Contributing Editor: Henrietta Wilkinson

Typeset in Great Britain by
Central Southern Typesetters, Eastbourne
Manufactured in Hong Kong by
Regent Publishing Services Limited
Printed in Hong Kong by
Leefung-Asco Printers Limited

PICTURE CREDITS

The Australian National Gallery, Canberra. Alias SRL, Milan. Artek, Helsinki,
Finland. Artemide GB, London. The Bridgeman Art Library. Christie's Colour
Library, London. The Crafts Council, London, and the craftsmen they represent.
Ecart International, Paris. E T Archive. Barry Friedman Ltd, New York. Collection
Galerie De Windt. Angelo Hornak. Toby Jellinek Private Collections. Knoll
International, London. Bernard and S Dean Levy Inc, New York City. Lusty Lloyd
Loom, Chipping Camden, Gloucestershire, England. Lusty and Sons, London.
Lutyens Design Associates, London. M W United, London, on behalf of Messrs Franz
Wittmann KG. Mallett and Son London Ltd. Partridge Fine Arts Ltd, London.
Phillips Auctioneers, London. New York and Bath. Sotheby's, New York. Spink and
Son, London. Stair & Co, London. The Storehouse Group, London. Numerous
Private Collections.

I am particularly grateful to the staff of Christie's and Partridge's; also to Barry
Friedman, Miss Hunt, Ben Jansen, Toby Jellinek, S Dean Levy, Sarah Lusty, Miss
Palmer and Mr Partridge, whose personal assistance has helped me greatly.

CONTENTS

INTRODUCTION

St Mark depicted in the Gospels of St Henry the Lion, a German gospel of 1175, sharpening his quill pen. He is seated on a medieval ecclesiastical throne, which has a 'dosser' or low back; they were frequently made of fabric stretched between the two uprights. The legs are very probably x-framed, hidden here by an embroidered cloth.

St Matthew (from the same illuminated manuscripts) shown writing his gospel on a high-backed throne probably of panelled construction. The banker or cushion rests on boards forming the lid of a box beneath, which could then be used for storage. These thrones were often placed underneath a fabric or wooden canopy.

Necessarily functional, furniture over the centuries has been subject to design styles that closely reflect both social phenomena (political and financial) and artistic tastes of different cultures. The widening of communications around the world and the rapid development of manmade materials during the course of the last two centuries have radically quickened the pace of change, but throughout that time, it is individual craftsmen and innovators who have played an essential role in refining and reassessing chair design.

From the earliest times, European chairs were divided into the purely functional turned or folding stool, and the more imposing throne for those in power – namely royalty, church and the law. Much of the furniture made before 1500 was of wood, and has therefore not survived, but evidence in paintings and sculpture shows that for the majority of the population in Europe at least, stools and benches were the norm.

However, refinement of design was clearly in force where there was money to be spent, and patronage of the arts and of craftsmen produced beautiful and functional chairs. As wealth became more widely distributed amongst the growing populations of Europe, a process greatly speeded by trade with the Orient and Europe's new colonies, and later by the far-reaching effects of the Industrial Revolution, chairs were in increasing demand. Delicate elegance, such as that seen at the courts of the French kings Louix XV and XVI, was in many cases sacrificed to comfort, practicality and economy in the Victorian years.

European furniture design periods have tended to be named after either the prevailing political climate, ruler of the time or after individual craftsmen: Chippendale, Hepplewhite and Sheraton for example. Similarly, André-Charles Boulle established (possibly invented) a technique of brass and tortoiseshell marquetry, much used during the reigns of Louis XIV and Louis XV.

Carving was the main form of decoration on wood, and continued to be so in the Gothic architectural movement and the Italian Renaissance. The Baroque movement, which also started in Italy, continued this penchant for carving, and the gilded and ornate work were the precursors of the Rococo movement. Although France was to take the lead in setting design tastes for much of the 17th and 18th centuries, individual craftsmanship was at its peak in England. Holland, too, had developed its own distinctive national style from as early as the 16th century. The Dutch were among the earliest to explore different types of wood from their colonies, and marquetry and veneer were highly sophisticated by 1700.

Developing trade between East and West had a considerable impact, widening Europe's artistic boundaries. Japanning, for example, was widely adopted in the 17th century; the term describes European lacquer techniques attempting to copy work imported to England. Similarly, Chinese chairs of the 17th century were clearly of an elegance as yet unseen in Europe.

Just as trade increased contact between different cultures outside Europe, so political turbulence was responsible for exchange of ideas within it. Religious exiles from France in the 17th century moved first to other European countries, taking with them their crafts, and then across the water to the newly-found America. The art of printing, too, meant that as early as 1580, Hans Vredeman de Vries of Holland could publish pattern books of his furniture. The 18th century saw a spate of pattern books from the great English cabinet-makers Thomas Chippendale (1718–1779), George Hepplewhite (d.1786) and Thomas Sheraton (1751–1806). This cross-fertilization of ideas increased in the 19th century as a vogue for international trade fairs (such as the Great Exhibition of 1851 at Crystal Palace) sprang up, and continued into the 20th century, with the important centres now expanded to include Milan, Philadelphia, Chicago and Vienna, as well as London and Paris. Wartime refugees to the United States sowed the seeds for the American postwar design boom.

The effects of the Industrial Revolution in the 18th century on chair design were immense. Larger and wealthier urban populations made new demands for space-saving pieces that provided comfort at a reasonable price. Machinery was developed that could take chair manufacture into new areas. Experimentation with metal tubing, chrome, plastics and fibre-glass have changed the face of chair design in the 20th century. The last two, for example, have led directly to the mass production of one-piece chairs, stemming from innovative designs by the Americans Charles Eames and Eero Saarinen in the 1940s. This revolutionary development produced a move away from decoration on chairs and towards fluidity of line.

This concern for line appears to be abating somewhat in the last quarter of the 20th century. Attention is focused instead on the widening division between unique and individual work from the designer-craftsmen on the one hand and the commercial demands of an ever-growing international market on the other.

BEFORE

1600

A Greek two-handled bowl of the 6th century BC decorated with a cock-fighting scene. The two spectators sit on folding x-stools known as diphros okladias, *a light portable seat that could be carried by a slave and set up when needed.*

A Greek amphora of similar date showing Zeus sitting on a throne with animal claw feet. Such chairs, derived from Egyptian or Asian originals, were used by the Greeks as seats of honour in theatres or other public places.

Before 1500, few Europeans (as we know them now) had even seen a chair, let alone sat on one. Earlier chair design had existed, however, and one of the earliest recorded pieces of surviving furniture is a folding chair of ash with a seat of otter skin, in much the same design as a 19th or 20th century campaign stool. Found near Muldbjerg in Denmark, it is believed to date from before 1,000 BC. But this piece is particularly unusual not just because of its early date, but also because climate has destroyed almost all wooden seat furniture made before 1500. Consequently, tracing the development of European chairs has to be through surviving paintings and art from over the centuries.

Surviving artefacts from the ancient Egyptian, Greek and Roman civilizations, for example, give clear evidence of contemporary seating. Chairs were standard practical equipment for the royal Egyptians – the Pharoahs were buried with several for use in the afterlife – and Greek and Roman drawings on vases and wallpaintings show that they were in common use then too, although virtually none have survived. Indeed, Greek provided the English language with words for both chair (cathedra) and throne (thronos), and during the neo-Classical revival of the late 18th century, attempts were made to reconstruct chairs from this time using the scant evidence available. The 'Klismos' chair in the Victoria & Albert Museum, London, is one of these.

In Europe, the use of formal seating was generally restricted to kings and bishops, the holders of power. Church influence on chair development is clear; what was possibly St Augustine's chair from the 6th century can still be seen at Canterbury Cathedral in England, and illuminated medieval manuscripts show Romanesque monks using chairs in the 12th century. England's Richard II is depicted on his throne towards 1500, and Leonardo da Vinci (1452–1519) painted Jesus' disciples on stools in his famous painting of the Last Supper. By 1550, boisterous peasants using stools in the fields appear in works by Bruegel, and just before 1600 Caravaggio places St Matthew in an identifiably X-framed chair in the tavern from which he is called to be converted.

Following the 13th century Gothic style, design sophistication before 1600 reached its heights with the Italian Renaissance, initiated in Florence. The joined panelling technique developed in Flanders c1400. The 'Savonarola cross' chair, a folding chair with a high back fixed with leather or panel, was relatively plain, but other chairs, stools and benches made of planks were carved into more delicate shapes. Walnut was mostly used, but documents from the period show that the Italians were employing as many as 30 different types of wood in their furniture making at this time. Further north, the heavier Gothic styles combined with the lighter Italian style to produce a rectangular mix of the two, typified in Hans Vredeman de Vries' pattern books published in Holland c1580.

The quality of 16th-century English furniture was not as high as elsewhere in Europe. Benches and tripod stools were used at meals, but chairs were reserve for the head of the household alone. Settles (benches with arms and backs) were large and more permanent pieces of furniture. Joint work developed, and in the mid 16th century, Henry VIII had started a trend of employing foreign craftsmen, many of whom produced magnificent walnut chairs in the 1540s. His daughter, Elizabeth I (whose reign lasted from 1559–1603) had chairs decorated with inlaid woods echoing the Renaissance styles dominant on the European continent, and seats were used in much greater numbers. Upholstery, too, developed, changing from the mere addition of a cushion to a wooden seat to a complete covering of the back and seat with tapestry and velvet.

PRE-1600

1. The State Throne of Tutankhamun, *c*3000 BC

This is a reconstruction of one of the earliest free-standing chairs. The original was excavated from the tomb of the Egyptian Pharaoh in 1922. Beneath the embossed metal and enamel it has a simple wood frame, basically identical to those found in most Western homes today. There are many good examples of Ancient Egyptian chairs and stools in the Cairo Museum, perfectly preserved because of conditions within the tomb.

Little is known about Greek and Roman chairs other than from the designs on contemporary vases and paintings; the next reliably dated examples of chairs are European, from the late Middle Ages onwards.

2. A 16th-Century English Four-Legged Stool or Table, *c*1580

The clover-leaf top of this piece is something of an enigma, and probably unique. It is certainly strong enough to be a stool and the carved columnar legs are identical to joint stools of the Elizabethan period. However, the top is relatively thin, therefore probably too weak to be a seat. Whether a chair or a table, it is very rare, very early and a very pleasing relic from the times of Drake and the Armada.

3. An Oak Joint Stool, *c*1580

This beautifully decorated stool is not only early but extremely rare. The arcaded rails are characteristic of the Elizabethan era, but in this case the arches were filled with a carved scallop shell; still seen on the end of the stool, although the others have broken, this was probably a unique feature. The fluted legs are also unusual in the way that the beaded ring forms the capitol; it is interesting to note how a typical Renaissance decoration is interpreted by the English craftsman. There may also have been an applied border of decoration in between the arches on the square-sectioned legs, forming a continuous arcade.

2

3

1

1600 TO 1700

A detail from a 17th century wedding scene by the Dutch artist Jan Steen, showing drunken revellers in a tavern. The woman on the right is sitting in a turned and joined three-legged chair with a hoop back. These were among the earliest types of joined chair developed in Europe after the Middle Ages. The man on the left has over-turned a rush-seated chair with spindle stretchers, turned uprights and a curved splat back. Such chairs were developed in the 17th century, but they continued to be made in country districts throughout the 18th and 19th century and it is not uncommon to find such basic and practical seating today.

Between 1600 and 1700 design changes were swift and clearly documented. The refinement which had begun in England and France in the mid-16th century continued, to such an extent that by 1640 chairs had appeared showing the influence of clothing fashion on their design. The Farthingale chair, for example, was armless, to allow women dressed in the voluminous costumes of the time (sometimes as much as 4ft/1m 22cm wide) to sit down. Politics, too, had a considerable influence, seen both in the plain, no-nonsense lines of Puritan Roundheads in England and in the refined design of the glittering court of Louis XIV of France at Versailles.

French style at the turn of the century showed good proportion, clear design, restraint in ornament and a high degree of refinement; workmanship was of the very highest order. Flemish and Italian craftsmen, imported into France at the turn of the century by Henry IV, had taught their crafts to apprentices, and within 50 years or so the French had outstripped their masters. By 1640, chairs were low-backed, as in Holland and England, those with high backs developing at court. In general, chairs were of simple design, and with finer turning in France than in neighbouring countries; their chief decoration was their upholstery.

In contrast Louis XIV furniture was opulent, classical, and highly symmetrical. The development of marquetry using brass and tortoiseshell (known as boulle since André-Charles Boulle established the technique in France) was just one of many decorative techniques developed during Louis XIV's reign. French court chairs of the time were generally carved in oak and polished or gilded softwood and were notable for their hierarchy: armchairs (fauteuils) or chairs without arms (chaises) were reserved for the king alone, a stool (tabouret) was a privilege for the courtiers, and folding stools were reserved for duchesses. In well-to-do private homes, upholstered armchairs and wing chairs were generally high-backed, with finely-carved arm supports and legs.

Oak was the dominant wood in English 17th-century furniture up to around 1660. Charles I had made efforts to align England with the arts movements on the Continent but the Civil War and 11 years of Puritan rule (1649–1660) had a profound influence on styles. Despite this, upholstery became more widely used during this time, and Elizabethan carving excesses were toned down. The development of regional chair styles suggests a wider use of seating than previously, as does the widespread production of the turned (or thrown) chair and the stick-back chair (now known as the Windsor chair). But it was Charles II's restoration to the throne in 1660 which made a dramatic difference to English design. The monarch's links with overseas tastes and craftsmanship during his years in exile were maintained when he returned to England, and flourishing trades – with apprentices – were soon well-established. Trade and overseas colonization created enough wealth to follow latest styles such as veneering (detailed work which required finer craftsmanship than anything before, and led to the emergence of the prestigious cabinetmaker) and lacquer work, based on the exotic oriental work being imported from the Far East.

An important cross-fertilization of ideas between England and the rest of Europe took place through the religious persecution of the French protestant Huguenots by the Catholic authorities. William & Mary (who came to England from Holland in 1689 to reign) invited the persecuted Huguenots, many of whom were master craftsmen, to take refuge in England. The new king and queen also brought with them several of their own outstanding craftsmen, one of whom was the renowned Daniel Marot. Consequently, by 1700 English woodworkers were working with the very latest in cabinetmaking techniques.

Furniture produced in America during the 17th century mainly reflected tastes and styles of the mother countries of the settlers. Indeed, furniture was scarce at the start of the century and few pieces remain, although at the time chairs with straight back-posts and rush seats were widely used: refinement was seen in the turning rather than overall shape. Towards the end of the 17th century, designs were filtering over from Europe, and especially England, but American Colonial styles remained very much their own, simpler and more functional than their fashion-conscious European counterparts.

So by 1700, there were gilt chairs in France, marquetry in Flanders, sculptural carving in Italy, regular trade between Europe and the Far East, and constant contact between Europe and the Americas. By the end of the century, the chair was no longer a symbol of power – it had become the seat of the populace.

1600-1700

4. An English Oak Chair, c1600

This unusual design is probably from the late 16th or early 17th centuries, and one of just a very few made. The notion of forming the back from an architectural arch is extremely original, and the details are strikingly carved. The Renaissance gave rise to a number of architectural details such as the 'arch' back supported on columns. This is a very English version, though, with little of the Italian elegance. The wear on the uprights and plain columns forming the front legs indicate an early date.

5. An English Oak Armchair, c1640

This chair certainly dates from the first half of the 17th century, since its proportions and construction are so typical of that period. It is most notable for its beautifully carved back, the design of which depicts a double-headed eagle with outstretched wings. The eagle motif forms part of the arms of Prussia, although these may be the indistinct arms of the northern English Speke family; early armorials and crests are often difficult to identify from mere decoration. The chair also bears the initials T.W., probably added during an owner's inventory. Still showing the influence of earlier throne-like chairs, this tall armchair is 3ft 8ins/112cms high.

6. English Inlaid-Oak Joined Chairs, c1650

Chairs such as these were made throughout England from the end of the 16th century, and are perhaps the first generation of chairs as we know them today. They take their name from the joiners who made them, applying the same simple construction to chairs as they did to buildings. The mortice and tenon joints are held together by pegs from the outside, quite clearly seen on these chairs at the bottom of the front legs. In the earliest examples, the members were heavy, with some decoration, and the stretchers almost touched the ground.

The chair on the left is fairly sophisticated, and although sometimes produced in walnut, this example is oak. Its back is decorated with carved scrolls on the arch and also has inlaid central panels with stylized marquetry flowers, probably using bog-oak, holly and other fruit woods. This chair also has turned legs, which lighten the legs at the front, and undulating arms.

Although similar, the other chair is probably from a slightly earlier date. It bears the initials 'I.T.', which probably refers to the owner of the chair, since coats of arms were rare at this time. The panelled back is in the form of an architectural Roman arch

6

7

4

5

surrounding a stylized vase of flowers of geometric fruitwood inlay. These chairs are likely to have been restored since they are of very great age, and some of the new pieces may themselves be over 200 years old. The seat rail and parts of the legs may be later, betrayed only by their slightly uncharacteristic look and lightness of wood.

Although oak is now less fashionable, it was once thought to be the most desirable of woods. Chairs and joint stools such as this from the 17th century were often forged and adapted with timbers. Forgers were extremely enterprising both in the 19th and 20th centuries, often burying timbers in bogs for years to give the right texture, dryness and colour. A good 19th-century fake may now be nearly 200 years old, so beware!

7. A Pair of Ming Dynasty Chairs, c1600

The Ming Dynasty lasted from 1368 to 1644AD, and these chairs probably date from the late 16th or early 17th centuries. The contemporary European equivalent would have been a throne or possibly an early caqueteuse. Although the caqueteuse also has a U-shaped back, these Chinese chairs are particularly harmonious, with gentle curves balanced by the out (the curving end of the arm). It is interesting to note that below the front of the seat the rail is carved with a scrolling pattern similar in some respects to the aprons on Georgian chairs. The construction of the back also resembles European chairs of this design, with a central splat (back panel) which is decorated. Chinese chairs are known in other forms from at least the 13th century AD, which suggests that the development of the chair in the East may have been parallel to that of the West, or, more likely, influenced European designs. This same design continued to be made in China well into the 19th century, also appearing with a square back. That the same basic design has been used for so long is a marvellous example of Chinese reverence for tradition.

8. A Pair of 17th-Century Chinese Stools

This pair of barrel-shaped stools with inserted stone tops could not be further removed from the European joint stool of the same date. These beautiful, flattened spheres in hardwood are made without a straight line, and their elaborate stretchers form an intricate design which resembles contemporary brocade patterns. The quality of the cabinet-making reflects the sophistication of Eastern civilization, and explains the fascination which boosted the Chinese export trade.

9. Two 17th-Century English Oak Joint Stools c1660

These two stools are part of a set of five period joint stools, of which there are only a very few known; to find even a matching pair is difficult. That this was a large set, presumably once six, is an indication of the fact that stools were the main form of seating, perhaps arranged around a heavy and similarly structured refectory table. They combine a lightly carved frieze with stout, reel-turned legs which are massive and cylindrical; there are similarities with the spindles on the thrown chair.

10. A 17th-Century Oak Caqueteuse, 1668

The French verb *caqueter* means to chatter, and this early form of chair is sometimes called a chatterbox chair. This lovely example is very solid, almost as if dug out of a fairly large piece of oak, and is beautifully carved with a perfect patina. The chair is small enough to be homely and inviting, and stands about 3ft 3ins/99cms high. Probably Scottish, it is very rare in being dated. It is interesting to see its influence reflected in the work of the Arts & Crafts chairmakers 200 years later.

10

9

8

1600-1700

11. A 17th-Century English Turned or Thrown Chair, c1675

Thrown chairs appeared very early and were widespread, extending beyond Europe. They are thought to be based on a Byzantine model, although many examples are found in Scandinavia. The earlier designs have triangular seats and are three-legged, similar to early joint stools. As can be seen, each individual component is turned on a lathe to form the desired shape and then fitted like a peg into the frame.

This wonderful sculptural object, with its lovely geometric rhythm, could easily have been made by a craftsman of 20th-century Vienna Secession. It is probably late 17th-century English, and is made from the traditional woods of oak and ash.

In England, the Guild of Turners can be traced back to the 14th century. One of the main functions of a trade guild was to ensure that specific work was carried out by its own members, although in provincial England, such rigidity was infrequently enforced: during the reign of James I, for example, the Shuttleworths of Gawthorpe employed a dish-thrower to make them a turned chair; as the name suggests, a dish-thrower made plates and bowls by turning them from wood, a practice which continued even into the 19th century. Clearly in Jacobean Gawthorpe, dish-throwers could turn their hands to anything, but in 16th-century Germany, where the Reformation banned the carving of religious images, the Guild of Carvers, who were consequently unemployed, were forbidden to carry out other carpentry work such as building.

12. A North Country Marriage Chair, 1675

The arched back rail as seen on this chair is a feature which is normally associated with the counties of either Yorkshire or Derbyshire, England. This chair has the added interest of three carved initials and the date. According to convention, the upper initial, M, represents the surname and the two lower initials are for the Christian names of the couple to be married during that year, 1675. This highly original chair would almost certainly have been a marriage gift.

13. Two 17th-Century Yorkshire Chairs, c1680

These two rather spectacular chairs are of a fairly typical 17th-century design. Solidly built, heavy timbers form the rails with mortice and tenon joints, and the front legs and cross stretchers are bobbin-turned to give a lighter look, although also retaining solid mortice and tenon joints. Their more remarkable aspect are their backs, which are typical of chairs from the Yorkshire area. Regional chairs, like oak furniture, are areas of study of their own. The scrolling finials on the uprights, combined with the characteristic double-crescent decoration, are very typical; so too is the vigorous carving in low relief with a variety of scrolling lines, and interlocking symmetrical monsters, seen here on the right hand chair. The designs remained fairly local well into the 18th century, and even into the 19th century in isolated areas. Presumably passed on from craftsmen to apprentices, they provided sturdy chairs for an undemanding market.

14. A 17th-Century English Oak Armchair, c1680

The armchair in its simplest form had fully emerged before the beginning of the 17th century, and had progressed from the box-chair, little more than a coffer fitted with a back, to this rather more sophisticated, joined piece. The structure remained essentially unchanged, however, and this chair is still massive in construction; consider, for example, the size and weight of the stretchers. There is little in the way of refinement here apart from a small frieze of carving along the top of the seat, echoed along the seat rail. New features can be seen, though; the arm supports and front legs are now baluster-turned, and the arms have some shape.

This chair could have been made as late as 1700, since rural areas often continued to use earlier, unrefined designs. That the chairs were functional and enduring is clear from the fact that they are relatively common today. Their production may well have continued alongside much fancier, lighter, pierced, carved and caned chairs of the period, which used less wood but needed more skill in their making. It should be stressed that at this time chairs were still fairly rare, and that most homes would only have had stools for seating.

14

11

13

12

15. A Pair of Late 17th-Century English Giltwood Chairs, *c*1680

The under-frames of these chairs are clear evidence of the French and Dutch influence on English design towards the end of the 17th century. The Huguenot craftsmen who fled the court of Louis XIV increased the taste for gilt furniture and for scrolling sculptural design. Similarly, Dutch craftsmen were imported with the Dutch Prince William of Orange when he arrived in England to become William III. Dutch influence on these chairs can be seen in the square-sectioned baluster front legs; note, too, the sculptural feel to the cross-stretchers which curve upwards into a pronounced scroll. The high backs, arched above and below, and the seats, are still covered with the original upholstery, a rich damask velvet with a frothy braid surround. It is possible to date these chairs to the last two decades of the 17th century, as they precede the cabriole legs and simplicity of design that began towards the end of the 17th century.

16. Two Louis XIV Walnut Armchairs, *c*1680

These two French *fauteuils* date from a time when chairs were becoming increasingly popular in Europe, and were being produced both in much greater numbers and of better quality. Note the beautiful turning on these barley-twist stretchers and arm supports, and the curving arms. They are in particular much lighter than previous designs, although still sturdy in appearance. In England, the chairs of Charles II's reign (1660–1685) imitated French design as the English monarch was keen to copy the court of the Sun King. These two, however, are fairly plain examples for their date, and are not especially courtly; they may even be from Flanders.

17. A Chinese Lacquered Armchair, *c*1680

Dating from the reign of the Chinese Emperor Kangxi, the unfamiliar design of this curious-looking low chair had a lasting effect on European furniture. Its construction is relatively sophisticated, lacking the rectangular frame of almost all European chairs of the same date, and using very few straight lines. This would have been built for an aristocrat in China, and has a heavy emphasis on decoration, less on supporting the structure, as seen in the pierced carving, a stylized representation of scrolling foliage.

The type of lacquer decoration seen here is traditional Chinese porcelain designs of the Song and Ming dynasties. It uses deep, strong colours and still conveys great natural beauty;

note the design on the seat. Europeans were already copying this type of lacquered work, although the concern with patterns made with interlacing curves and piercing was not approached in Europe until the height of Chippendale, a century later.

18. A Charles II Walnut Chair, *c*1680

With the restoration of the monarchy after England's Puritan Commonwealth in 1660 came an emphasis on decorated style. Charles II reigned from 1660–1685, and design during this time was particularly influenced by the craftsmen of the European continent generally, and by those of the court of the Sun King specifically.

This beautiful example shows traces of a plainer English tradition, seen in the turning of the rails which support the back, but is ornamented in the new style. Typical of the period is the caned back, and so too are the explosive crestings on the top of the back, the cross-stretchers, and the slightly absurd scrolls at the front of the chair. Until the contemporary design explosion of the 1960s, the 'old fashioned' carved scrolling which this chair epitomizes was considered the height of antique quality. It is still a splendid chair.

18

16

20

17

15

19. An English Oak Chair, c1685

This chair beautifully demonstrates the influence of the English Jacobean style on previous, more traditional furniture designs. The heavy oak frame is lightened by the use of thin rails and bobbin turning, and the solid top rail of the back is carved with prolific foliage in low relief; more courtly chairs of the time, however, would have higher relief carving. It is unusual to find a dated chair of this period without initials, which would indicate the owner, but this chair is simply a bona fide exception since the date and design match so closely. Both this enigma and the curiously balustraded back make this a most interesting chair.

20. A Pair of Late 17th Century Walnut Chairs in the Style of Daniel Marot

This pair of William and Mary chairs clearly shows the results of the prevailing foreign-influenced decorative style in England, c1690. Inspired by the Court of the Sun King, the Dutch monarch on the English throne, and an example of reaction against the plainness of the English commonwealth period which ended in 1660, the chairs are sculptural and operate on a three-dimensional level. This is seen clearly in the decorated backs, in the bold cabriole with inward scrolling toes, and, between these two, in the decorated stretcher below the waving seat rail.

The linear scrolling of the back panels depicts a fruiting vine sprouting from a classically shaped vase. The side stretchers, also boldly carved, typically join the back legs with square-sectioned mortice and tenon. The overall busy effect is typically 'Marot'.

During this period of history, England greatly benefited from religious strife abroad in the form of the Huguenot flight from France. French Protestants had enjoyed freedom of worship for about a century in Catholic-dominated France, since the Edict of Nantes. In 1685 this was revoked, giving Protestant ministers a fortnight to leave the country; any lay Protestants attempting to leave were condemned to the galleys or, in the case of women, confined to a convent. When William and Mary came to the throne in 1689 they issued a declaration inviting the French protestants to 'transport themselves into this kingdom . . . All French protestants that shall seek their refuge . . . shall have our royal protection . . . and being in this realm may be comfortable and easie to them.' This declaration was genuinely motivated by religious sentiment, but was also extremely shrewd, for the Huguenots were noted for their skill as craftsmen and for their

21

19

20

industriousness – the original Protestant work ethic. Daniel Marot was born in Paris around 1660, studied under Le Pautre, and was influenced by the work of Boulle. As a Huguenot refugee, he entered the service of William, Prince of Orange. By the end of the century there were over 20,000 Huguenots in England, working in every field from hatters to bankers, as weavers in Spitalfields and even in the 'Western suburbs' of Soho. Through Marot and his fellow refugees the splendours of the French court were introduced directly to the English court and to London life. His elaborate engraved designs dominated fashion well into the 18th century, a tradition continued by the *Pelletiers* (carvers and gilders) and James Pascall. Pascall's elaborate suites for the house at Temple Newsam, near Leeds, produced in the middle of the century, were very like the work of William Kent.

21. A Pair of 17th-Century Indo-Dutch Hardwood Armchairs

These intriguing variants on the style of James II chairs were manufactured in the Dutch East Indies, or Indonesia as it is today. Taking a European model, the attempt to copy it, possibly to capitalize on cheap foreign labour, resulted in a similar skeleton with very different flesh. The fundamentals are the same, with the barley-twist columns and stretchers, the foliate end 's' on the arms, and the caned seats, which in any case derived from the East. The difference comes in the carving. In Europe, the panels, particularly the crested top rail, the splat and the pierced stretcher, would have been of Renaissance cherubs with urns sprouting flowers. Indonesian craftsmen, however, were unlikely to have seen a European cherub holding an urn, and therefore carved dragons, lions and elephants amongst lotus flowers and trailing tropical plants.

It is a charming variant on the European tradition but beware ! – the Far East, including Indonesia, is still famous for carving hardwood forgeries ranging from William IV to 17th-century styles, all to order. They represent a serious pitfall to the collector.

22. A William and Mary or Queen Anne Walnut Chair, *c*1690

The most striking feature of this chair is its characteristic bulb-turned legs and the cross-stretcher. The turning of the legs tapers to form a central baluster while the contrasting curves of the stretchers produce an elegant pattern. This form of leg is a curious combination of prevailing continental influences with an enduring love of turning; a similar combination can be seen on the thrown chair and joined stools of the period.

The overall appearance of the chair may seem quite plain, but it might well originally have had brightly-coloured needlework upholstery acting as a foil to the walnut below, as on a similar chair in the Victoria & Albert Museum, London. The style of leg used here appeared for only a relatively short period of time, either in its plain form, or sometimes as a much more angular carved and gilded baluster; it was soon replaced by the more popular cabriole.

23. A William and Mary Painted Armchair, *c*1690

This rare example of a gilt and blue-painted William and Mary chair, with its original upholstery in very good condition, came from Godmersham House in Kent. Most striking with this armchair is its sculptural element: the arm supports and legs are elaborately carved with their edges heightened in gilt, and the front legs take on the form of herm shown with cherubs, a common subject for the many marble statues that might have been found in baroque gardens of the period. Note also the decoration on the arms, known as egg and dart moulding, another direct application of an architectural detail to furniture. Although more restrained than the work of Andrea Brustolon who created sculptural chairs on the continent, the influence of European craftsmen is overwhelming, and it clearly shows the richness it brought to English furniture design.

24. A William and Mary Lacquered Armchair, *c*1690

This chair, one of a pair, is particularly significant as it is one of the first design revivals to be seen in England. This model was originally produced in 1600, and is similar to one of that date from Knole, Kent. Knole, a stately home near London, retains most of its original 17th-century furniture, and has England's best collection of early chairs. From the Duke of Leeds' collection at Hornby Castle, York, there were originally six chairs

22

25

24

23

and at least one stool. It is an indication of the progression in chair design during the 17th century that by 1700 chair-makers were ready to re-think earlier forms, having achieved the complexities of twisting columns, caned seats, carved stretchers and even winged chairs.

This example in the scarlet and gold lacquer of the period is distinctly three-dimensional; the top of the chair back echoes the shape of the legs, and contrasts with the upturned bow of the seat. Despite looking back to the designs of the past, the stretchers which join the legs are beautifully baluster-turned and square-sectioned, a feature which very much belongs to the end of the 17th century. This product of adventurous designers confident in their sense of line, and in the technique of their craftsmen, heralded the great period of English chairmaking – the 18th century.

25. A William and Mary Walnut Miniature Chair, *c*1690

It is extremely rare to find a miniature chair of this period, but this example seems to have all the authentic characteristics of a full-size one of the same date: the outstretched arms, the scrolling front legs, the square-sectioned back legs and the arcaded front stretcher. The original needlework of anglicised oriental design was clearly executed by someone who had never visited the Far East. Measuring less than 18ins/46cms high, it was probably too small for a child to sit on and might have been for a doll.

1700 TO 1800

The Hall of Mirrors at Schloss Nyphenburg. Mid-18th century German rococo reached heights of unrestrained fantasy which surpassed even the French. The combination of light, colour, texture, pattern, asymmetry derived entirely from natural forms extends from the furniture to the bird in the 'sky'.

Although France was without doubt the dominant influence over taste at the beginning of the 18th century, different political climates did produce their own styles. Rococo was the style of the time with veneers, marquetry, ormolu mounts, and oriental lacquer. In France, two main styles of chair prevailed, the *siège meuble*, immovable and set against a wall, and the lighter *siège courant* which could be moved as and when required. Armchairs had their arms set back to accommodate the hooped dresses of the period, and lounging became popular so the sofa and *chaise longue* developed accordingly.

Rococo was at its height around 1730, characterised by asymmetry and organic forms such as rocks, shells, scrolls and foliage. A notable feature of the time was the exchange of ideas between different nations, leading to Dutch influence on English work, japanning in Italy, and traces of Chippendale and Queen Anne in Spain. George III chairs were closely imitated in Denmark and Hepplewhite shield backs could be found in Naples.

In England, the period 1690–1715 produced a return to sobriety in decoration – the basis of the Queen Anne style with higher-backed chairs and with vertical lines and plain splats. Then came the Georgian period of furniture (1714–1830) which found its main medium in the mahogany imported from the West Indies, c1725, overtaking walnut in popularity by 1750. The use of mahogany encouraged a return to carved decoration, and this can be seen in the work of Thomas Chippendale (1718–1779) the most famous of English cabinetmakers. His pattern book, *Gentleman and Cabinet-Maker's Director* of 1754, spread his fame throughout Europe and the world, and indeed the publishing of pattern books in the 18th century was a main cause for the movement of styles across Europe.

The second half of the century saw a move in Europe towards a neo-classicism. Robert Adam, a Scottish architect, followed in the steps of William Kent (1685–1748) as an architect concerned with the interior decorating of his buildings. George Hepplewhite also published a pattern book *The Cabinet-Maker and Upholsterer's Guide*, published in 1788, whose elegant, well-proportioned furniture is a fair representation of taste in the latter half of the century. By the end of the 18th century, English chair designs were imported, copied, adapted and widely admired in countries throughout the world, from America to Russia, and Norway to Spain.

With Louis XV's succession to the French throne in 1723 came the lighter, more elegant rococo style. When in turn Louis XVI and Marie Antoinette came to the throne in 1774, the flat surfaces and linear shapes decorated with lacquer and ormolu drew heavily on classical influences. The 1780s saw a vogue for English design; mahogany was introduced on a larger scale; neo-classicism and rococo merged until the traumatic Revolution of 1789. From then till the turn of the century saw the plainer Directoire furniture.

The growth of industry and trade in America by the start of the 18th century meant an increased exchange of ideas with Europe. The William and Mary easy-chair at the start of the century began to merge with more sophisticated Queen Anne designs around 1725, and American Queen Anne chair design showed the style at its best. The variety of skills required in chair-making (upholstery, carving, turning and joining) reached their height in Philadelphia in the mid-18th century. The influence of Thomas Chippendale arrived in America around 1760, and his name is synonymous with rococo in American design.

The American Revolution interrupted the flow of ideas from Europe, but Robert Adam's designs provided the base for the Classical Revival seen in the United States after the Revolution from around 1780 onwards.

New England Chippendale is much more linear than English Chippendale, and different areas show distinct stylistic characteristics. In Newport for example the mid-century furniture trade was dominated primarily by two families named Goddard and Townsend who incorporated many Queen Anne features into the New French Style. The pilgrim's shell motif became a recurrent theme carried from Queen Anne through to Chippendale furniture, particularly the striking block-front cabinet furniture. Newport Chippendale is often a more heavily decorated variant of Queen Anne; elsewhere in New England are strong stylistic variants, such as the work of the Dunlap family in New Hampshire who specialised in a rather anarchic use of the shell combined with a mixture of styles. Philadelphian Chippendale dominated the immediate area of the Delaware River, Maryland and New Jersey. In New York the influence was less pronounced. In terms of manufacture, the towns of Salem and Boston, tended to produce rather slender, vertical styles, though of a construction which necessitated the now outmoded stretcher.

Regional differences in Chippendale chair design are complex and well documented. They are a fascinating study but beyond our scope here.

26. An American William and Mary Bannister Back Chair, New England *c*1710

This fine example of American baroque is beautifully carved, with its pierced crest on the back, vase-turned legs and bulbous stretcher all forming contrasting tight curves, as do the out-turned 'Spanish' feet. Clearly an American version of a William and Mary chair, it is probably by John Gaines of Ipswich, Massachusetts. Other chairs of this set are in the Metropolitan Museum of Art. The Bannister Back chair gets its name from its balusters. Made of a mixture of woods, including maple and ash, a similar armchair in the Henry Ford Museum, Michigan, is ebonised; English chairs of the same design can be seen at Knole, in Kent.

American William and Mary style became popular during the first quarter of the 18th century, approximately a generation later than in Europe. Seventeenth-century Puritanism lingered, and few American chairs of the style are as elaborate or outrageous as European examples. They do have common features, however, notably turned stretchers and bannister backs, particularly those from Rhode Island. The Delaware River Valley also produced good turned chairs, often of plain woods with ebonized and painted decoration and complex turning. Another distinct style to become popular all over the United States was the Boston Chair. This usually had a leather splat which curved in towards the back in a similar fashion to English Queen Anne 'Chinese' examples. All of these different chairs generally used the mortice and tenon joint, sometimes with good bulb-turned stretchers.

It can be hard to distinguish between American and European chairs of this date. American designs use slightly different proportions, variations in decoration and raw materials, and have a greater simplicity.

27. A pair of Queen Anne Japanned Chairs, c1710

The form of these chairs, compared with the decorated style immediately before and after this date, is delightfully simple and draws elegance from the oriental designs which it emulates. It is very rare to find such chairs in good condition, since the frame of soft wood, probably beech, was often ravaged by time, and English lacquer was water-soluble and quite brittle.

The chairs' curves are very gentle, with the elegant cabriole legs giving outwards as much below the knee as above, thus creating a restful balance which ends on a simple square foot. Note how the back sways to fit the sitter, and how its broad central splat is decorated with oriental motif; surely an inaccurate attempt at a Chinese painted scroll. The anglicized Chinoiserie is evident on the seat rail also, which is scattered with various objects from the Orient – fans, baskets and so on – and the leaves on the legs are painted rather than carved, as might be expected on later Georgian chairs.

28. A Queen Anne Oval Walnut Stool, c1710

Although similar to rectangular stools of the same date, the oval seat in this example adds immeasurably to the harmony of line. Traditional English stool design of the highest quality, the curves of the seat are convex in contrast to the concave curves of the stretcher, and the out-turned feet are plain and dignified. An enchanting feature of this stool is that at the joints, where traditionally English blocks give way to a stretcher of undulating shape apparently inspired by oriental designs of the period. The stretcher is carved with a tobacco leaf of such simplicity that it is almost stylized, resembling the foliage on oriental porcelain imported during this period. The combination of such natural form and controlled curves on this disciplined design shows the touch of a master. The period needlework, with its graphic pattern, highlights the pattern of the undercarriage.

29. A Queen Anne Walnut Stool, c1710

The primary virtue of this early 18th century stool is its simplicity. Although at this date it might have been made as a stool on its own, it would probably have accompanied a suite of chairs. Its construction was sufficiently robust to be able to dispense with the stretchers, and this made the design far less cluttered. The legs taper elegantly to a slightly pointed pad foot, which has the simplest of line decorations. The simple linear motif on the knee of the cabriole is reminiscent of the decoration of contemporary silver, known as 'cut-card work' and from that line, flanked by a pair of scrolls, it hangs in a single husk. This particular needlework seat is later than the date of the original stool, but it would have had a similar design, which complemented the rich colour of the wood.

27

26

28

29

30. A Queen Anne Walnut Shepherd's Crook Armchair, *c*1710

This chair is as beautiful as it is unusual. Shepherd's Crook armchairs, a well-defined model of distinctive pattern, were produced primarily in the first quarter of the 18th century with some minor variations. This good early example still has stretchers, and in fact an unusual crinoline stretcher, supposedly designed to accommodate the dresses of the time. The simple tapering legs with pad feet and delicate blocks are typical late Queen Anne or early George I. As can be seen, this is little more than a stool with a superstructure added on. It is particularly pleasing in this case to see the period embroidery seat. The looped arms that give the chair its name; made in two pieces, they are joined by a figured simple walnut back.

31. A Queen Anne Child's High Chair, *c*1710

This functional child's high chair stands at just over 3ft/91.5 cms high, and would have seated a relatively wealthy child at table. Made primarily of walnut, the elms side rails are turned and square-sectioned, allowing a strong mortice and tenon joint; chamfered back legs are an extra sign of quality. It is authentically constructed like a full-size chair of the period, although it is made more robust by its extra cross-pieces. The undulating apron and simplified arms are nice touches and the slight wear on the foot rail conjures up scenes of the generations of infants who may have fed here.

32. A Régence Walnut Armchair, *c*1715

Régence describes the period 1715–1723 in France when the Duc d'Orléans was acting as Prince Regent for Louis XIV. Interestingly, it corresponds to the first few years of George I's reign in England and shows how French furniture developed during the reign of Queen Anne. As we have seen in England, Queen Anne's reign was a period of harmony, restraint and simplicity in chair making. There was a reversal of the trend towards decoration which characterized William and Mary's reign; in France, however, late 17th-century styles matured smoothly during the first quarter of the 18th.

This fauteuil, one of a pair, has many 17th-century continental characteristics; for example, the curving x-framed stretchers, the cabriole legs, the hoofed feet and the gently curving arms.

The open arms and contrasting curves give the chair a light, airy feel, and this effect is

30

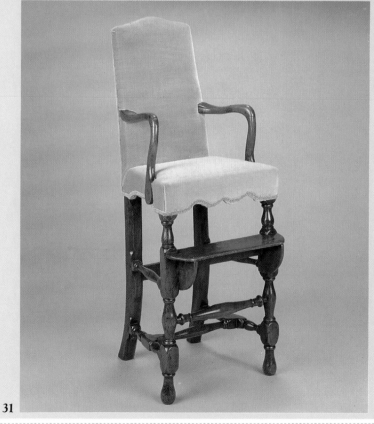

31

32

heightened by the high decoration; the scallops on the arms are echoed by the scallops and trellis work on the seat rails. There is also an extra finesse in the scrolled feet which rest on their own feet below. The mellow combination of the warm-coloured walnut against this tapestry upholstery represents an elegant high point in neo-baroque European furniture.

33. A Queen Anne Walnut Embroidered Wing Chair, c1710

Here, as with other examples of Queen Anne chairs covered in elaborate embroidery, the eyes are attracted to the pattern of the upholstery rather than to the woodwork or overall shape. The embroidery themes can vary from biblical scenes to simple scrolling floral patterns which lead off the edge of the chair, or local traditional pastimes; in this case the hunt. The simple cabriole legs immediately indicate the chair's age, as they are almost identical to those on the rectangular Queen Anne stools of the same date. The square-sectioned cabriole leg at the back adds an overall balance to the chair, and although disguised by the needlework, the outward scrolling arms and billowing wings which come from the high back are typical of this period.

33

34. An Early 18th-Century Georgian Wing Chair, c1720

It is difficult to be precise about the date of this chair but by comparison with the Queen Anne wing chair from the same period, these front legs are more highly decorated, with shell moulding, slight scrolls and have squarer feet. These back legs are much simpler than the front ones, perhaps indicating poorer quality craftsmanship, or perhaps a later replacement; this could only be determined by examining the frame beneath the upholstery. It is similar to the Queen Anne version in having the same high back, curving wings and outward scrolling arms.

35. A George II Red-Lacquered Chair, c1720 and a Pair of Round-Backed Chairs by Giles Grendey

Lacquering, or japanning as it is also known, reached its height of popularity and excellence in England during the first 30 years of the 18th century. Of the many workshops manufacturing and decorating in these styles at the time, Giles Grendey (1693–1780) is the craftsman best known today. He has given his name to this style of English lacquering which includes characteristically Anglicized oriental figures. Grendey established for himself a dominant share of the profitable export market in English lacquer, notably to Spain and Portugal. He was working at a time when British craftsmanship was at its height, and his empire grew to generate new trading partners. Grendey also made furniture in walnut and mahogany as well as small, neat pieces elaborately decorated with idiosyncratic motifs and shaped panels. English lacquer was generally of higher quality than that of the Dutch, a main rival at this time.

During the 1730s, Grendey supplied a suite of lacquer furniture similar to this chair (35a) for the Spanish Duque del Infantado to furnish his castle at Lazcano, near San Sebastian in northern Spain. There are also similarities to a set of four dining chairs at Godmersham Park, Kent, which have similarly-designed cross-stretchers, back legs and shell motif. (Godmersham Park is thought of as one of the last great chair collections to be broken up.)

In spite of many illustrious associations, Grendey was a furniture maker for the well-off English middle-classes rather than the aristocracy. His life was a combination of ambition and idiosyncracy. He was apprenticed in 1709, and by the 1720s had already taken on his own apprentices (whom he seems to have treated with great cruelty). In 1747 he became upper warden of the Joiners Company, describing himself as a

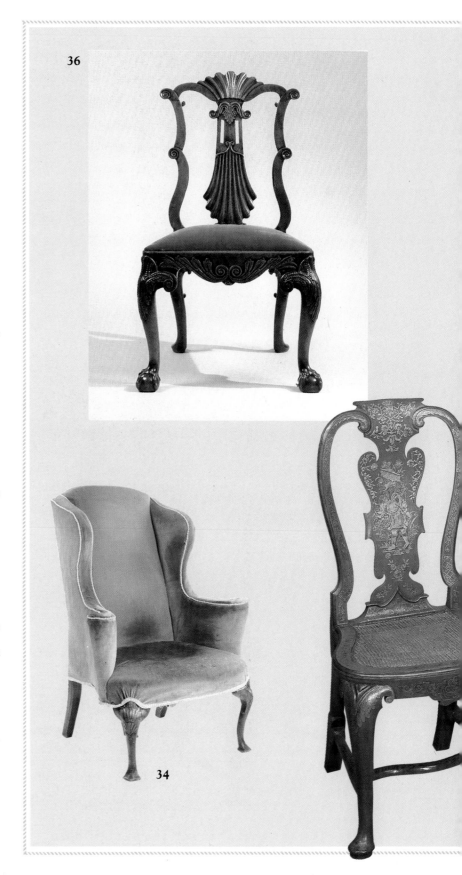

36

34

35a

35b

cabinetmaker in St John's Clerkenwell, London. By 1766 he had become Maitre of the Company, but was admonished the very next year for poor attendance.

He is perhaps best remembered for the enthusiasm with which he promoted scarlet lacquer furniture, which became a symbol of opulence and quality. As examples of his different styles, and to explain the attribution of these chairs to his workshop, it is interesting to compare the figures on the splat of the high-backed chair to those on the vase splats of the more homely, round-backed examples (35b) which are similar to a set at Temple Newsham, near Leeds. Both scattered with English-looking orientals, which came to be his trademark, in fact the overall effect bears little resemblance to an oriental scene; perhaps therein lies the charm.

36. A George I Mahogany Dining Chair, c1720

This original and striking design has been attributed to the hand of Thomas Chippendale's father in the past, but there is little evidence to substantiate this: it perhaps resembles the work of Giles Grendey (1683–1780). The legs and seat are of a standard type though the carving is excellent – the detail on the leafy knees adding great texture – and the back is quite extraordinary. Its two flat side rails resemble something between a lyre and a sabre, and flank the highly imaginative splat. This affecting combination of lightness and baroque vigour is difficult to surpass.

37. A George I Walnut Sidechair, c1725

This one of a pair of early chairs has two interesting features: its back and its carving. Although each side of the back is made up of two opposing scrolls, there is a high degree of horizontality about the design as a whole, and even the corners of the scrolls are sharp and angular, as is the splat. This emphasizes the horizontal lines in what is essentially a vertical arrangement, and gives the impression of extra breadth which was very characteristic of early Georgian design. These were broad, solid, chairs with an unrockable stability about them.

The chair's carving, on the other hand, is distinctly baroque. Consider the maskheads on the knees of the legs: these are not naturalistic, but nature is used simply as the model or inspiration behind the decorative lines. Later in the century the move towards rococo and truly organic forms led to lighter and more realistic carving, which often carried less impact.

38. An English George I Walnut Gilt Chair, c1725

This chair is from an important set which is now divided between the Metropolitan Museum of Art, New York, and the Colonial Williamsburg Museum, Virginia. It is a spectacular example of a really good walnut chair; beautifully carved, the back with small and expressive scrolls, a large expansive seat, and decorated with gilding, which is extremely rare. The chair has an undefinable exuberance which is rarely equalled.

39. An Early Georgian Stool or Bench, c1730

Although this stool may appear at first to be unusually low, it is in fact of normal height but is designed to seat more than one person, which makes it rare. The wonderful legs are the height of contemporary style, powerful lion-paw cabriole with a splendid rococo cartouche on the knee, surrounded by a variety of foliage on splendid, hairy ball-and-claw feet.

39

38

40. An Early Georgian Walnut Dining Chair, c1730

The tall, slender back of this beautifully carved dining chair indicates that it probably dates from George I's reign. Its exceptional feature is the elegantly carved lions' heads on the knee of each cabriole foot. These are distinctly naturalistic, and this kind of realism was a typical English characteristic which gave carving tremendous life.

41. English Cock-Fighting or Reading Chairs

Probably from the late George I or early George II period, this delightfully eccentric chair (41a) stands out amongst all others because it is used back to front, is also a table and, as in one of the examples, has a drawer, or sometimes hinged flaps or trays. The flap can be adjusted to place the book or paper in the right position, and the flush, lockable drawer in the front rail and flaps which swing out from the sides would have held writing materials such as quills, quill cutters and pounce pots.

The lack of stretchers and decorated cabriole legs suggests that the chair with the drawer is from the 1730s. The tightly-curved edges of the rounded seat tapering to the back, and the padded yoke, are very typical of the early 18th century. The studded leather upholstery is also period, and the stout pad feet kicking out at the back give the chair a robust feel.

It is interesting to compare this chair with a later example (41b). Here, the yoke and back are no longer padded, the back is reeded in late 18th-century manner, the lines are severe, and even the kicking-back legs are restrained. The later design has none of the assertive confidence of its ancestor; its lines are carefully measured and restrained, but there is a loss of elegance in the loss of simplicity.

Very sculptural and very English, there seems little evidence to link these chairs with cock fighting, although the back-to-front pose is often seen in contemporary paintings of the sport.

42. A Shepherd's Crook Armchair, c1730

A later example of a Shepherd's Crook armchair with a more interesting shape of back. Note too the absence of stretchers. This style of chair was also revived in the 19th century.

41

41a

40

42

43. An Early Georgian Shepherd's Crook Armchair, *c*1730

The Shepherd's Crook arm of this chair is a fine example of the style, and is fitted to what is probably the carver from a set of dining chairs. The flatness of the rails and scrolls is typical of the George I period. While it is a three-dimensional chair in that it is high, deep and shapely, each individual element is carved in one plane only; for example, the splat scrolls outwards but not backwards or forwards, and likewise, the top of the cabriole leg is flat and stylized, not at all naturalistic. It is as if it is made of a variety of pieces of card which are cut out into silhouettes; it has an excessive, over-decorated look and may be of Irish origin.

44. Two George II Walnut and Burr Walnut Dining Chairs

These excellent examples of chairs of this period are part of a set of eight, which had by then become standard. They display many clear features of George II chairs; note especially the beautifully figured burr splat of double-baluster form, with diminutive scrolls which match those on the ends of the arms. The veneers, chosen from cross cuts of the tree, have been carefully matched. The front legs carry the Astley family crest and are scrolled above hairy paw feet, and the back legs kick out to a simple pad. It is interesting to note the dimensions. While the armchair is of normal height – 3ft 4ins/101 cms – its width of 2ft 8ins/81 cms is unusual, making it almost cubic in proportion. The generous seat was designed to take the full coats of the period.

45. A George II Mahogany Irish Elbow Chair, *c*1730

This chair has many qualities associated with Irish craftsmanship in the 18th century. Although basically English in design, there is an overall heaviness in the combination of shepherd's crook arms and elongated back, in the slight disproportion of height to depth, and in a surfeit of carving, which often accompanies Irish work. Even though the back legs are somewhat clumsy, the chair shows the charm of Irish Georgian furniture, especially with its original petit and gros point needlework seat which sets off the deeply-coloured wood.

Generally Ireland, like other English colonies of the time (particularly America), followed prevailing English styles and adapted them to local taste. Ireland did not enjoy the prosperity brought about in England by the Industrial Revolution. Design advanced much more slowly, and therefore George II styles, such as this chair, lasted well into the reign of George III; in turn, severe late Georgian chairs continued to be made further into the 19th century than in England.

46. A George II Walnut Shepherd's Crook Armchair, c1740

This armchair exhibits every type of George II decoration. Originally one of a set of six, one is now in the Victoria & Albert Museum, London, and four are at Clandon Park in Surrey. The back is a fairly typical shape, formed from scrolls but crested with a delightful spray, like a peacock's tail, which sits above a solid, vase-shaped splat, inlaid within a strung border. The arms are in the shape of a shepherd's crook and the legs are cabriole.

What really makes this chair exceptional, however, is its carving. The legs are carved with open leaves which look a little like scallop shells, hung with closed leaves, and the foot really resembles a scroll of paper. There is a fan-shaped anthemion on the seat rail, and to lighten the overall effect the seat, still covered in contemporary needlework, is upholstered in bright and white tones.

45

44

47. A George II Love-seat and Two Single Chairs from a Suite of Mahogany Seat Furniture

This excellent suite, originally from Aspley House, Bedfordshire, comprises a pair of love seats and six chairs. They are from the great period of English chairmaking, and the fundamental structure of the pieces contained with their scrolls characterizes early English rococo. The love-seat pictured here is an example of a form which reached its height in the first half of the 18th century. It was certainly a social form of furniture, falling between the large carvers of this period and the double chairback settee; the ideal frame for an intimate conversation in a formal salon.

The large C-scroll, which forms the back and ends just above the seat, is carved all over with rocaille and acanthus. The splats are similarly decorated in low relief around the central interlacing strapwork: this baroque motif continues throughout the century. The arms of the love-seat can be seen to be carved both outwards and then in, and also upwards and then down. The front legs are cabriole with a cabochon on each knee, terminating in hairy hooves. The beautiful red brown tone of this early Cuban mahogany is quite irrepressible: colour is one of the most crucial determinants of age.

48. An American Queen Anne Walnut Chair, c1740

Interesting to compare with the other Queen Anne chairs illustrated, the shell carving, general shape and cabriole legs of this Philadelphian chair are very similar. The scrolls on this chair, however, have an extraordinarily sinuous effect and the splat is finely figured to create a delightful combination of simplicity and decoration. American Queen Anne chairs clearly mark the development of an indigenous style. In New York (originally, of course, New Amsterdam), elaborate baroque Dutch style tended to produce rather bulbous splats and an abundance of foliage carving, particularly on the crests, whereas in New England, and particularly Massachusetts, British conservatism favoured a vertical look with higher backs and often with a stout rear stretcher between the legs. (There is a good example of a Newport chair in the Winterthur Museum in Delaware.) Oriental lacquer became increasingly popular and there are some notable Queen Anne chairs with slightly elaborated European-Oriental decoration. Thomas Johnson, who described himself as being 'Japaner at the Golden Lyon in Anne Street, Boston', was notable for this kind of work.

49. Two George II Mahogany Dining Chairs, c1740

These beautiful chairs are from a set of two armchairs and six singles which originally also had stools and triple-seat settees. Good examples of George II dining chairs, the first notable feature is the excellent colour and figuring of the wood, striking even in a photograph. The second is the tremendous virtuoso carving, particularly of the seat and top rails. It is deep, crisp and luscious, embellishing its undulating seat rail; this shape of seat rail is sometimes known as the Vitruvian Scroll. The armchair's unusual combination of curved timber forms a pattern of interlacing lines, giving these large chairs a light and elegant appearance. Even if the baroque decorating is exaggerated, these examples of early rococo are a credit to the ingenuity and craftsmanship of the time.

50. An English Provincial Chair, c1745

While of beautiful quality, when this chair is compared to the London chairs of the same period, it seems a little gauche. The carving, for example, fails to reproduce convincingly the form of the swags of cloth it is trying to represent.

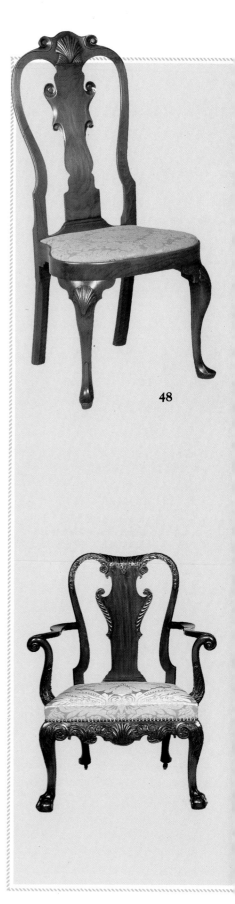

48

50

47

47

51. A George III Giltwood Armchair, c1750 by the Cabinetmaker William Gordon

This chair is from part of a considerable suite of 30 armchairs, four sofas, 16 single chairs, two stools and a waisted library table made for Spenser House in the 1750s. The suite represents the epitome of mid 18th-century taste and style, derived by a traditional partnership of the patron (in this case the first Earl of Spenser), and a designer (John Vardy) who directed the overall look. Vardy duly commissioned the great cabinetmaker William Gordon to make the chairs.

Although William Gordon primarily worked with another craftsman, John Tait, in a firm of cabinetmakers which operated in the 1760s and 1770s, he had already made a mahogany suite at Althorp similar in design a decade before. He subscribed to Chippendale's *Director* (1754), a hugely influential source of inspiration to the furniture trade. The firm of Gordon and Tait appear in several London Directories at various addresses, two of which were in Little Argyle Street and in Swallow Street. Between 1770 and 1779, there are several detailed bills for work at Althorp and also at Wimbledon. The partners later divided; Tait continued working in Piccadilly for the Royal Household during the 1790s.

The suite is representative of mid-century English rococo, a style which remained more constrained than the European styles. Here, the rails are curved, the legs cabriole on scrolling feet, and almost every surface is extensively carved.

52. A Windsor Chair, c1750

The term 'colonial furniture' broadly refers to pieces made before the American Revolution of 1776. Prior to that date, design influences came from two main sources, England, and Europe generally. Each nationality of immigrant – the Dutch perhaps most influentially – imported not only furniture but also a traditional affection for that style; the styles combined to give rise to recognizably American-made designs, particularly after the Revolution. American-manufactured chairs, even more obviously than English ones, fall into two categories: rustic, which by definition were the chairs that most Americans used, and formal, more rigorously based on popular styles and particularly imported ones.

The Carver Chair is a good example of Jacobean American, based on a chair which was supposedly brought over by John Carver, the first Governor of the then British colony. The chair has a typically English 17th-century, slightly baroque, look. The Brewster chair is an elaborated version of the same

design, and both were used as models, widely copied in a variety of woods – oak, cherry, hickory and walnut. This Windsor chair is clearly related to its English cousins. The Ladderback Country Chair, which appeared in England and on the European continent, often with a rush seat, also became Americanized for everyday use, and is still made by the Shakers today. It should be remembered that many of the first immigrants to sail to America were fleeing religious persecution (such as the Pilgrim Fathers) and were generally Puritans wishing to avoid Catholic oppression. Their Puritanism is reflected in generally plain designs and an inherent conservatism.

53. An American Queen Anne Chair, c1750

This elaborate example of a Rhode Island chair shows clearly the change in style from heavy, earlier forms to this light backed seat; it has a slender splat, but still retains its heavy stretchers. The change can be seen too in the style of carving on the knees, the pendulous ball-and-claw feet with the claw at the back, and the crested top rail with a fan shell, this last in the style of Englishman Giles Grendey.

54. An American Queen Anne Walnut Chair, c1750

This exquisite example of simple Pennsylvanian design with typical shell decoration is probably by Philadelphian James Bartram, who was the original owner and from whom it had passed to his descendants until sold in New York in 1985. Bartram was listed in 1726 in the Delaware County Deedbook as a joiner in the Marple Township; it is extremely rare to find a chair with such a history on the open market. Particularly remarkable are the delicate cabriole legs ending in what are known in the United States as slipper feet and which show a marked French influence when compared with the stern, strong, English back.

54

53

52

51

55. A George II Giltwood Armchair, *c*1750

This is one of a superb suite of eight armchairs and a sofa (56) originally at Rudding Park, near York. It displays all of the best aspects of English rococo, with a design openly indebted to the style promoted by the court of France's Louis XV. It is quite small and light (3ft 4ins/101cms high), and the arms are upward swept on leafy scrolls, echoed on the four cabriole legs which terminate at a scroll at the toe. The rails are serpentine-shaped and carved with leafy decoration in relief, with central cabochon and all the varieties of rocaille decoration. The rich effect created by this gilt underframe is countered by the severe shape of the upholstery, giving an overall balance to the chair.

56. A George II Giltwood Sofa, *c*1750

This sofa comes from the same suite as the armchair from Rudding Park, near York. It is interesting to see how the rococo is translated into a larger piece of furniture. It is expansive (8ft 8ins/264cms wide), and although it has the structure of chairs joined together, with eight legs altogether, full use has been made of the sculptural possibilities. The back, arms and feet scroll effusively in every direction exhibiting a freedom which the chair, being full, heavy and more baroque, does not enjoy.

57. A George II Mahogany Settee, *c*1745

This good example of an English rococo sofa is light and elegant; even the padded seat is slender, perhaps not as robust as others. The expanse of the back, and its squareness, is moderated by the gently waving sides; the woodwork is of a high quality too, beautifully carved with typical scrolls, and delicate cabriole legs. Typical of English rococo, the sofa is not excessively decorated and forms a suitable companion for a suite of chairs because it would not dominate the set excessively.

55

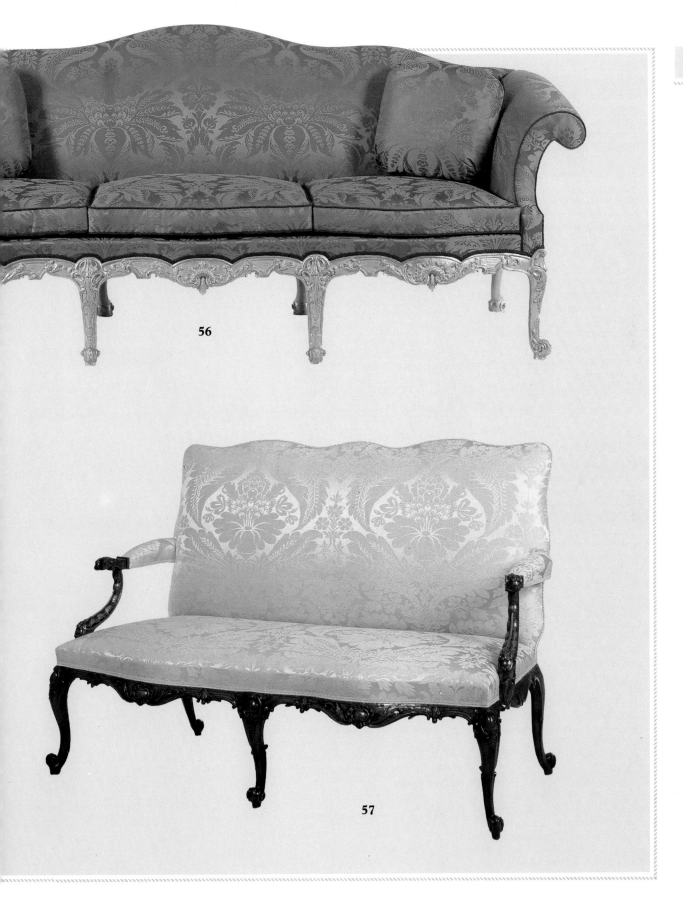

56

57

58. A Pair of George II Mahogany Chairs

From the transitional period between the early Georgian solid, carved and decorated look, and the later George III light, linear and elegant pieces, the style of these chairs sows the seeds for chair design of the second half of the 18th century.

Here, the backs are still fairly flat, with broad rails and a broad central splat; the splat is pierced with a symmetrical design, a rococo element, and the uprights are straight, giving a slimmer look which is lightened by carving. The legs are still cabriole, and carved on claw-and-ball feet, but are much longer and lighter than their predecessors. The seats remain balloon-shaped, but the rail is shallow with only an ear remaining of what was previously a bold, undulated wave. The period embroidery provides a sharp contrast to the dark and more sober frame.

With very minor adjustments these remaining curves could be straightened to make the whole effect rectangular and severe: it is possible to see Robert Adam and George Hepplewhite beckoning from the future.

59. A Philadelphia Chippendale Chair, c1775

These chairs are part of a set, part of which is in the Winterthur Museum, Delaware, US, a house originally used by George Washington. Made in the American Chippendale style (although not based on drawings from Chippendale's *Director*) they were produced in America during the same period of 1750–1780. They are primarily mahogany but also include some poplar and pine. Most striking is that they are excellent examples of Philadelphia carving, which can have a dazzling, almost expressionistic, quality. Although the motifs are based on nature, they appear as tight, parallel curves or outward-moving lines which are very striking.

Philadelphia was the second largest English-speaking city in the world in the mid-18th century. Its output of furniture polarized American furniture production between Pennsylvanian and New English design. The popularity of decorated European styles was greatly accelerated by the arrival of Thomas Affleck from London in 1763. He worked with Philadelphians such as William Savery, James Gillingham, John Shoemaker and the celebrated Benjamin Randolph. American Chippendale indulged in more curves and sculptural form (such as the universal ball and claw feet) than the English Chippendale style, and indeed sometimes seemed more continental than English in flavour. Like their English predecessors, the pieces tended to be on a large scale, and especially those from the Delaware River Valley which are sometimes rather plain, in the Queen Anne spirit. Shoemaker and Savery both produced chairs with wonderfully undulating rails and sometimes retained the crisply-carved shell motif, again an anachronistic Queen Anne motif. Around 1770 Randolph produced a set of sample chairs which are full-blown rococo, or as it was frequently described, in 'the new French style'; these have Gothic tracery to the backs, bow-shaped top rails, pronounced cabriole legs on scrolling toes, a rare feature, and all manner of carving. The chairs are now in Colonial Williamsburg Museum in Virginia, US, which like the Winterthur Museum in Delaware, has an excellent selection of chairs of this period. The link with central Europe is particularly in evidence in Pennsylvanian rustic furniture with its bias towards decoration, whether on the painted German marriage chests, the naïvely carved hall chairs, often clearly decorated on the homestead by amateurs, or the dozens of other country designs drawing on influences as diverse as the Tyrol and the Italian Renaissance.

60. A Mid-18th Century Chair-Back Settee in the manner of Thomas Chippendale, c1750

This design is a classic of its kind, and it is interesting to compare it to the George II love-seat illustrated earlier (47). Little more than two chairs joined together, it is notable for its elegance, rather than its comfort. The 'chairs' are typical Chippendale, with elaborate, interlaced, ribbon backs, leafy back rails, and all on gothic, triple-column front legs. Much of the woodwork is ornamental rather than structural. Consider, for example, the small corner struts between the legs and the front rails; in the form of a Gothic, crocketted arch, they give style but little strength.

The importance of this design is that it is a stepping stone between the love-seat and the fully upholstered sofa that we have today. This settee design could be adapted to be two, three or four chair-backs long and in spite of its slightly comic, three-legged appearance, it is an important step in the development of seat furniture.

58

59

60

61. A Chippendale Wing Chair, c1750

This interesting variant in the progression of the wing chair combines traditional characteristics and original ideas in a particularly Chippendale way. Although still sculptural, it is different to a Queen Anne chair in that it is much squarer; the wings resemble those of 17th century chairs, which were often hinged, and with arms scrolled upwards instead of outwards.

Here, however, legs and stretchers indicate the age quite clearly. Harshly rectangular, the only curves to be seen are the decorative struts between seat rail and leg. These features are distinctly English, bearing no resemblance to the open armchairs of the 1730s and 1740s which were much influenced by France. The reintroduction of the stretcher is a curious characteristic since stretchers had ebbed in popularity since the early 18th century, but it was perhaps necessitated by the lighter frame, or perhaps solely for decoration.

62. A Pair of George II Gainsborough Armchairs, c1756

These fine examples of mid-century comfortable armchairs by John Gordon (62a) were of a style supplied to a number of great houses at the time. There is a set of eight of these chairs at Blair Castle, Scotland, also known to have been made by John Gordon of Swallow Street, London, in 1756; he was of the Gordon family of the firm Gordon and Tait who were also associated with the gilt Spenser chairs. The original documentation at Blair describes, 'eight mahogany chairs carv'd frames in fish scales with a french foot with a carv'd leaf upon the toe.' They cost just under £4 each.

Although they are of the same comfortable proportions as armchairs today, they are of unusual design. The arm supports down to the seat seem to emulate a dolphin motif found on contemporary French and Italian chairs, here delightfully understated. The seat rail, in the form of a Cupid's bow, alludes to classical motifs of an earlier period and sweeps down into the simple cabriole with the nicely detailed leaf. The fishscale decoration is also from the organic baroque vocabulary of the earlier century, and the reeded edges and restrained lines of the upholstery show wider European ideas adapted to English taste. There is an obvious similarity between these chairs and the hall chair pictured (62b) also by John Gordon.

63. Two Georgian Mahogany Armchairs, c1756

This spectacular pair of armchairs is from a suite of seat furniture based on a design by Thomas Chippendale. Similar chairs are illustrated in his *The Gentleman and Cabinet Makers Director*, Third Edition, published in 1762. The chair backs appear on Plate 10, and the chair rails and legs on Plate 13. These highly original chairs are possibly the most sculptural examples of 18th-century English chairs, and show the possibilities that the Chippendale pattern books presented.

A good example of a Rococo suite, these chairs fall between Grotto furniture (which has backs and seats based on shell forms) and early George II, heavily-ornamented neo-Baroque chairs. Note the carved coat of arms in the back – those of Bassett of Tehidy Park, Cornwall. These chairs were made for Sir Francis Bassett who married Elizabeth, daughter of Sir John St Aubyn, in 1756, 20 years after Tehidy Park was built.

64. Two Chinese Chippendale Chairs, c1760

These are good examples of a type of chair known as Chinese Chippendale from a set of twelve from Elvden Hall, Norfolk. Here, the term 'Chippendale' is used in the broadest sense, for these are not after a design by Thomas Chippendale. As can be seen, the chairs bear very little resemblance to actual Chinese pieces, which to this day remain more or less the same as the oriental chairs illustrated earlier. Here, there are strong elements of Gothic decoration on the arches on the splat. This style reached its height between 1750–1770, and produced some very elegant chairs.

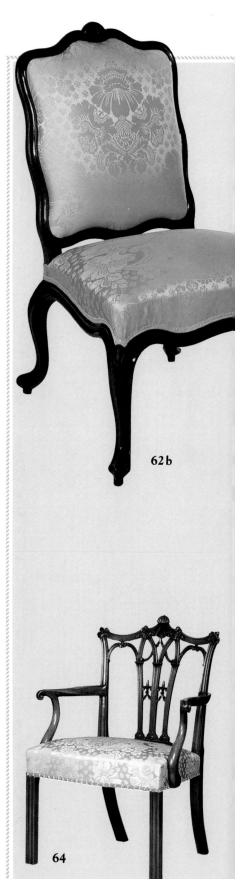

62b

64

65. An American Queen Anne Armchair, *c*1760

The term 'Queen Anne' as used here refers not to the reign of Queen Anne, nor the English style of that time, but to the style popular in America during her reign at the beginning of the 18th century. It corresponds more to the European William and Mary style; note the bow-shaped top rail, and the many curves in the chair's outline. The chair was probably made by John Elliott of Philadelphia, and shows three beautiful examples of the American scallop shell motif. A curiosity of this chair is that the inscription on the back of the crest spells OIL, probably for Oliver Ingraham Lay, a New York, 19th-century artist who obviously had a reverence for the antique, but was not too shy to adapt a piece for his own satisfaction.

66. A Pair of Gothic George III Windsor Armchairs, *c*1760

These are classic Windsor chairs made of elm and yew in country style, upright and sturdy. Windsors often adopted prevalent styles of the period in which they were made, and these are Georgian Gothic Revival. Just as Horace Walpole transformed his country house at Strawberry Hill outside London by changing the façade with the addition of Gothic battlements, towers, and other Mediaeval paraphernalia, so Gothic architectural details are used here to make these chairs seem Mediaeval. The backs are in the shape of a Gothic arch, and the splats echo the Gothic tracery pattern to be found in cathedral windows. These are nothing like real Gothic furniture which consisted of little more than primitive stools and rough tables.

67. A Louis XV Single Chair, *c*1760

This is one of a set of 12 single chairs by Nogaret of Lyon. With its curved sides and elegant cabriole legs, it is the epitome of French elegance of the time, envied and copied all over Europe, and especially in England, which dominated the chair market throughout the 18th century. Although graceful and shapely, the chair decoration is more discreet than much Louis XV, marking a move towards more sober tastes.

66

69

67

65

68

68. An American Queen Anne Walnut Armchair, *c*1760

This Philadelphian armchair is the product of some of the best craftsmanship seen before American Independence. The curvaceous design with a dramatic top rail is loosely based on chairs from the reign of William and Mary in England; the splat and cabriole legs are early Georgian; and the reeded lines carved on the edge of each rail are a unique adaptation of a Queen Anne idea. The construction is substantial without being heavy and the effect is sculptural, although not as excessive as some English George II chairs are. The beautifully figured splat and carved shells are delightfully American.

69. A Giltwood Bergère, *c*1764

This impressive bergère, the French term for an armchair with upholstered sides, was probably made by Jean-Baptiste Tilliard the Elder who worked between 1740 and 1760. While it still shows some rococo curves, the basic chair shape is being straightened to become more expansive and cubic; a little more neoclassical. It is on this type of bergère that Robert Adam and other English designers based so many of their own versions.

It is interesting to notice the variation in style of arms found on bergères. They are sometimes the same height as the back, forming a kind of tub, or can be much smaller as here.

1700-1800

70. A Louis XV Giltwood Chair, *c*1765

This chair, now one of a pair, would have been part of a salon suite, which may well have included sofas. It was made by Jean-Baptiste Tilliard who came from a well known family of Parisian *menuisiers* (joiners). He became a maître in 1738 and was attached to the Garde-Meuble for several years before founding his own workshop in 1741. He supplied the French court with chairs and various other pieces of cabinet furniture. The elder Tilliard retired in 1764 but his son, Jean-Baptiste II, took over the workshop and continued to make furniture into the reign of Louis XVI.

This chair is absolutely typical of a style established in the first half of Louis XV's reign (1723–1774) and which has been popular ever since. The fundamental structure of the frame is a series of serpentine curves which form the seat rails, the sides of the backs, the legs and the arms. The back, which is rectangular, gives the impression of solidity and stability. The combination of white paint and gilt had tended by this time to replace the pure gilt of the luxurious first part of the reign. This is a basic example of the model which the English adopted and which set new standards for elegant solidity.

The French crown throughout the 18th century had a voracious appetite for furniture to decorate the great palaces; Tilliard, Jacob and others were the suppliers and, in part, promoters of the French style.

71. An American Chippendale Chair, *c*1765

This chair, made in New York, clearly shows the influence of English Chippendale and has many characteristics from Chippendale's pattern books. There is the New York balance between decoration and plainness, its roots in the designs of the original Dutch inhabitants, but it is also moving towards an increasing Anglicization.

This chair was made for one Elias Boudinout of New Jersey.

72. Two George II Mahogany Dining Chairs, *c*1765

Taken from a set of 14 by Robert Manwaring, one could be forgiven for looking at these chairs and shouting 'Chippendale'. Chippendale has come to mean mid 18th-century mahogany furniture of this type, although not pieces necessarily by Thomas Chippendale, or from his workshop. Robert

Manwaring designed and probably actually made the chairs. In 1765 Manwaring published *The Cabinet & Chairmaker's Real Friend & Companion* and the following year *The Chairmaker's Guide*. From these we know more about his work than about him, though we know he was active in the 1760s and specialized in chairs.

Manwaring's design is generally rather more solid and 'masculine' than that of Chippendale. Certainly, this furniture has a frontal appearance. The rails are broad and flat, and the effect is not lightened by the fretwork carving and attempts to orientalize the design. While rather earthbound compared with Chippendale, these are really excellent chairs.

73. A pair of George III Mahogany Stools, *c*1765

This well-known model of stool is probably based on a design by Thomas Chippendale. Generally of good quality and with examples distributed right across the country, this style originated from the 1760s. There are 26 of them in the Christchurch Upper Library at Cambridge University, which are believed to have been supplied by Thomas Chippendale in July, 1764. The fact that they are in the library clearly indicates that they are seat furniture and certainly not foot stools, fulfilling the same function as sets of joint stools in the 17th century, and upholstered stools at the beginning of the 18th century.

The elegant bowed seats, in the form of an extended scroll, are standing on unusual, curved legs joined by a Gothic arched stretcher with a central patera. Stark in comparison with earlier upholstered stools, they are an interesting combination of Gothic and rococo scroll, and like other furniture of this period, tend towards severity. It is interesting that a similar design is found in a set of painted rococo hall furniture at Petworth House in Sussex, which shows their flexibility of function and appearance. An aquatint of a library from Ackermann's history of Oxford and Cambridge universities shows stools of a very similar design.

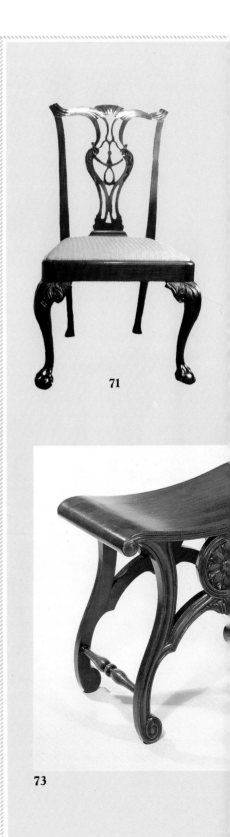

71

73

72

70

74. A pair of George III Mahogany Sidechairs, c1770

It is interesting to see this unusual integration of the armorial escutcheon painted in the centre of the interlacing reeded straps which form the back; in addition the family crest is carved into the toprail. Although the painting of family arms on chair backs, or carving them on the knees, is not uncommon, it is usually on the solid backs of hall chairs which were traditionally made in pairs or sets. Although these appear to be from a dining set they have very shallow seats and so may have been intended as very elaborate hall chairs. The slightly top-heavy proportions which derive from their transitional style. The rectilinear backs are in contrast to the Hepplewhite shield form. They have as many broad horizontal lines as vertical, giving a massive appearance. The weightiness was necessary to support the central plaque. The legs and rails are crisply carved which reduces their mass, and serpentine to reduce the impact of the horizontal; the tapering to a waisted foot makes the uprights seem longer. The heavy back on a lighter base typifies the transition between heavy and light Georgian.

75. A Philadelphia Chippendale Sidechair, c1770

This splendid chair is crisply carved on a plain strong design, all lightened by the cabriole legs and the interlacing pierced back, which is taken direct from Chippendale's *Director*, Plate XVI (lower right), published in 1762, which shows how rapidly English influence penetrated abroad.

The chair was one of a set made for Charles Thompson, Secretary of the Continental Congress during the American revolution, and there are four very similar sets, one of which is in the Winterthur Museum, Delaware, US. This chair, with its fully documented history, represents the peak of American mid-eighties furniture taste, and fetched a world-record price in 1987 of over US$250,000.

76. A pair of George III Giltwood Chairs, c1770

This pair of chairs belongs to a large suite of 12 chairs and a sofa from the collection of the Hon. Mrs Aileen Plunkett, from Luttrellstown Castle, Dublin. Made in the 1770s, these chairs are relatively restrained compared with the large, French-influenced, Louis XV pieces so popular at the time. Even so, the gilt legs are ornate, with anthemion sprays and an unusual looped swag decoration

above the fairly straight cabriole legs. The appeal of these chairs is that the legs contrast with and thereby heighten the effect of the simple lines of the upholstery.

These chairs can be compared to a suite of giltwood armchairs supplied by Chippendale for the Couch Room at Harewood House, Yorkshire. The Harewood chairs are even more neo-Classical in taste, and both are good examples of the parallel inclinations towards simplicity and decoration which mark the period.

77. A pair of Hepplewhite Mahogany Armchairs, c1775

These are one of the most elegant variants of a style known generally as Hepplewhite, although they do not necessarily appear in George Hepplewhite's own pattern book. The shield-shaped backs are particularly lightened by the carved details at the top, and by the vase-shaped frames containing a notional fleur de lys motif. The legs are fairly standard, tapering to give a slimming effect, and the feet are smart sabots. Most spectacular are the arms: beautiful wide loops which are probably too high for practical use but add a kind of bravura elegance. The neat appearance of the chairs comes from the pattern of lines formed by the frame; by curving back in to themselves rather than jutting outwards, they give the chairs a calm, lyrical balance, even if in practice they are neither comfortable nor robust.

78. A Pair of Philadelphian Chairs, c1775

These are not only an excellent pair of Philadelphian chairs by the well-known maker Thomas Tufft, but they are perfectly documented. They were part of a suite which were entered into an account book by Richard Edwards of Lumberton, New Jersey, US, who recorded purchases both for his General Store at Lumberton and for his own household. The Chippendale suite comprised a high chest of drawers, a dressing table and this pair of chairs. The Edwards-Harrison family sold them in 1987 for US$ 1.76 million.

78

76

77

75

74

79. An English Giltwood Armchair, c1770

This chair, now one of a pair, was formerly part of a suite from the home of the Dukes of Argyll at Inveraray Castle, Scotland. It bears all the hallmarks of French taste which so influenced English chairmaking during the third quarter of the 18th century; compare it, for example, with Tilliard's Louis XV giltwood chair (70). Both are substantial, with large expanses of flat, rectilinear surfaces, and both are lightened by the elegantly curving rails and legs. Here, the decoration on the rail is particularly refined, emphasizing the serpentine shape with reeding (the small moulded line at the edge of the rails); this increases the rails' apparent length. The line is continued past the indented knee to the scroll toes, balanced on their own peg-top feet.

80. A Provincial George III Dining Chair, c1770

Provincial chairs of this date differed from their London-made cousins both in the material, which is not mahogany, and in the pattern. Although the shape is similar, this chair, for example, lacks refinement of carving and the light, strong framework. It is slightly heavier in appearance and retains the outdated square legs and stretchers. It is possibly by a provincial chair-maker following a London pattern: consider, for example, the motif resembling a scroll on the top corners of the seat back. The cabinet-maker seems to have followed the pattern without understanding that this should resemble a piece of scrolled paper, having never seen an original. This chair would originally have been part of a suite.

81. A Chippendale Dining Chair, c1765

This interesting chair from a set of 12 originally came from Kippax Park, Yorkshire, and is probably by the Yorkshire firm of cabinet-makers Wright & Elwick of Wakefield. Both partners in the firm were known to subscribe to Chippendale's *Director* and this is similar to many of his designs. The two partners worked together between 1745–1771; Wright probably came from London to join Elwick, a man of plain tastes. Together they founded a firm which dominated cabinet-making in northern England throughout the second half of the 18th century.

82. A pair of English Gilt Armchairs, c1765

While rococo began to wane in Europe, in England it was at its height, as is seen in the third edition of Thomas Chippendale's *Director*. This pair of armchairs are two of the best of their kind, with exaggerated curves, heavily carved with rocaille, and with a pronounced cabriole at the back. Although fundamentally rectangular, they have used as many of the exaggerated rococo curves as the English dared. To some, this is an acquired taste, but it is still worth admiring these chairs for their excellent craftsmanship.

83. An American Chippendale Wing Chair, c1770

This chair could easily be English, although documentation proves that it comes from Newport, Rhode Island, US. It is in spirit very close to English Queen Anne Wing chairs; the upholstered parts are the same shape as those of its English cousins and the cabriole legs have claw and ball feet joined by turned stretchers which end in substantial blocks. This frame is in mahogany, whereas the English Queen Anne chair would probably be walnut-framed. The stretchers of this chair are delicately turned, like the spindles on some American Windsor chairs, and the ball and claw carving is typical of Rhode Island. Its date of 1770 shows the conservative American affection for earlier styles, as it is some 50 years behind English designs. The title 'Chippendale' here refers to the Chippendale taste popular at this time in America.

84. An English 'French Hepplewhite' Bergère, c1770

This English-made chair is typical of the new style imported from France, which emphasized comfort as much as the look of the piece. Designed to support an ample frame, the arms have become a part of the back, and it is easy to imagine a Georgian *bon-viveur* collapsing in one of these in the library after dinner. These are the forerunners of the English tub chair, and are clearly different from the open armchairs and wing chairs which had preceded them.

80

79

84

83

82

81

85. A Pair of Chairs by Georges Jacob, c1770

Similar to the pair of Jacob chairs illustrated, these bear the *ébéniste's* (cabinetmaker's) stamp on the woodwork beneath. They would originally have been gilded and were perhaps stripped during a change of taste away from their elaborate cousins from Jacob. Naming chairs with a maker's label or stamp became increasingly popular throughout the 18th century, particularly in France after 1750, and toward the end of the century elsewhere: it has continued until the present day.

86. George II Gilt Armchairs in the style of Robert Adam, c1780

These handsome chairs were taken from Powerscourt, County Wicklow. They are archetypal Adam, with their oval backs and nicely-carved back legs. The unupholstered example here shows both the construction of the chair and the type and age of wood used. The frame is the only part not covered in gilt or, in the case of mahogany, polish; it should be just like this – dry and hand-sawn with a light, mellow look to it. The seat rail is joined to the legs by invisible mortice and tenon joints which are screwed or pegged at the corners for added strength (although used here, pegs were considered old-fashioned by this date and were often discarded after 1750). The oval back was probably made in four pieces, again pegged for strength. The nail holes on the frame shows where the stuff-over seat had been fixed. This oval back panel had been nailed to the frame, though on European chairs, it was often fixed with a catch and removable, a practical detail which shows a kind of refinement rarely seen on English chairs.

87. A George II Mahogany Dining Chair, c1785

This chair came from a set of 12, which could also have originally had two armchairs with it. Good examples of quality Hepplewhite suites, the design may well have come from his famous pattern book *The Cabinet Maker & Upholsterer's Guide* of 1788, published two years after his death. Hepplewhite was an apprentice of Gillow of Lancaster and his somewhat conservative pattern book epitomized the furniture of the 1780s and 1790s, utilizing classical motifs in a restrained, English way. Although, according to Ambrose Heal who wrote on English furniture makers, 'his contemporary reputation as a maker was in no way exceptional,' he gave his name to a style of furniture of lasting appeal, regularly reproduced even today.

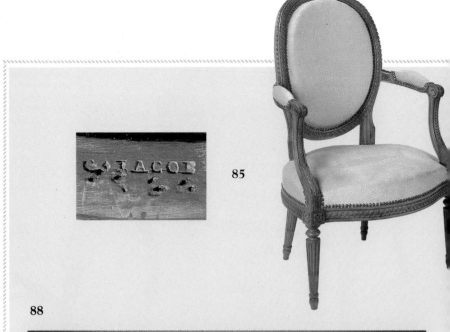

85

88

Hepplewhite laid claim to the three Prince of Wales' feathers motif as being of his own invention, even though it was in general use at the time. The shield-shaped back, however, is very much Hepplewhite's style, as are the serpentine-front seat rail and tapering, reeded legs.

88. An American Chippendale Wing Chair, c1780

The Queen Anne style continued to be popular well into the American Chippendale period which dominated fashion during the second half of the 18th century. This is very much a transitional chair; the upholstered parts resemble traditional Queen Anne chairs, with high backs and outward-scrolling arms, whereas the visible frame (the legs and stretchers) are very much Chippendale, with straight lines and of square or rectangular section. The front legs are fluted, an architectural motif revived in furniture design by Robert Adam. After the War of Independence, America very swiftly re-established contact with, and reproduced, European fashions. It is known that Chippendale's pattern books were available, and designs such as this were popular alongside earlier Queen Anne styles.

86

87

89. A Pair of Louis XVI Giltwood Armchairs, c1780

These classic late 18th-century French chairs came from a suite of six *fauteuils* (covered armchairs) by Georges Jacob; broadly speaking, the style corresponds with that of Robert Adam in England. The two craftsmen shared an architectural spirit and taste for classical ornamentation as applied to these salon chairs. Just as Adam was one of the great chair designers, Jacob was one of the great furniture makers, specializing in chairs. He was not only an *ébéniste* (cabinetmaker) but also a *menuisier* (chairmaker or joiner).

Born in Burgundy in 1739, by 1765 he had become a *maître ébéniste* and his reputation soon spread. From 1773 onwards he received numerous commissions from the crown, and in 1781 he was appointed *ébéniste ordinaire* to Monsieur le Comte de Provence (who afterwards became Louis XVIII). He was one of the great French cabinet makers and his work is well represented in the Louvre, the Palais de Versailles, and at Fontainbleau in France, and in the Victoria & Albert Museum and the Wallace Collection in London. (The latter is one of the finest collections of French furniture and works of art.)

The general horizontal feel of the chairs comes from their breadth, and from the backs roughly forming square panels. All the rails are profusely decorated and carved: neoclassic architectural friezes, a ribbon twist around the main rail, the beading on the arm supports, and fluting on the tapering legs.

90. A Louis XVI Giltwood Sofa, c1780

Made by Georges Jacob, the constant tension between elaborate decoration and control, as seen here, was common to all Western European designs during the 18th century. This sofa has an enclosed, sheltering quality which is emphasized by its curves. The controlled carving of interlaced ribbons forms a constraining border for the plush interior, and the sofa is supported by an unobtrusive set of stubby legs. It is interesting that, although a later replacement, this fabric is identical to that used by Louis XV, and is actually from the same source.

Jacob, who was extremely versatile, was himself influenced by English standards, presumably of constraint, and at Windsor Castle there is a suite bearing his stamp in distinctly English taste. He was also known to use ungilded mahogany with an effect reminiscent of English brown furniture.

91. A George III Mahogany Armchair, c1785

This unusually elaborate armchair has an intriguing combination of motifs. The pierced back is carved with a most unusual splat of a central urn above an anthemion with interlaced ribbons. The front legs are distinctly Adam, and the arms have an elegant pronounced scroll in the French taste, clearly showing the fashionable influence of the time. However, the classical urns and architectural references are details imposed on what is basically a carved English chair.

92. A George III Mahogany Dining Chair, c1790

This would originally have been the armchair from a suite of anything from six to 32 chairs; generally, most of them would have been single with one pair of armchairs such as this. Relatively plain and undistinguished, they are still elegant, with the rectilinear back decorated only with stretchers of opposing curves, making the chair light and serviceable. It is the arm supports and turned-baluster legs which indicate a date towards the end of the reign. These were clearly extremely popular; and there are many mid-range chairs of a similar pattern readily available today. Because of their popularity, designs such as this were produced well into the 19th and 20th centuries.

93. A Sheraton Painted Armchair, c1790

This is a classic example of late 18th-century beechwood furniture. Typical of the type illustrated in Thomas Sheraton's pattern book, published in the early 1790s, its frame is a basic shield-shape with various motifs forming the splat. In this case, two arrows either side of a tall chair and a laurel wreath are all tied by a ribboned bow. The rest of the frame is painted with swags, husks and other piecemeal decorations from Thomas Sheraton's repertoire. It is very characteristic of the elegant, classically-inspired patterns of this time, with an added sophistication in the black painting and extra colour. Although nowadays these chairs are found singly or in pairs, they were originally supplied in reasonably large sets. Their design marks one of the peaks of late 18-century decoration. From this point on, they began to be over-decorated and thus excessive in a heavily coloured and textured room.

93

90

92

91

89

94. A Pair of Anglo-Indian George III Ivory Chairs, c1790

Since the 17th century, the Orient acted as a valuable source of exotic materials. While lacquer is associated with China and Japan, the abundance of Indian elephants provided a plentiful source of ivory of the whitest colour and the purest texture. During the late 17th century, Anglo-Indian furniture consisted mostly of cabinets and caskets of local woods, such as ebony and coromandel, inlaid with figurative and geometric designs. At the start of the 18th century the move toward austerity during the reign of Queen Anne halted this trend, and furniture of the mid-century was primarily carved from mahogany from the Western Empire, especially Cuba and Honduras. Towards the end of the 18th century, more elegant designs and the taste for dramatically-coloured furniture brought forth a variety of small ivory-veneered objects such as tea caddies and games boxes, often with the stained decoration characteristic of the industry based in the province of Vizagapatam.

India under British rule produced some veneered furniture based on contemporary British designs. Often with slight variations, these were veneered in ivory rather than being solid mahogany, rather in the style of walnut veneers of the early 18th century. However, these particular chairs are solid ivory. Of considerable weight, the Hepplewhite-style frame is painted with orientalized gilt foliage. They could almost be mistaken for cream lacquer, and are clearly associated with the white-painted furniture and lacquered chairs of the end of the 18th century, which in turn heralded the exuberant Regency taste of Thomas Hope and George Smith.

95. Two American Federal Armchairs, c1795

These armchairs are unusual in being American Louis XVI, which was fashionable before the French Revolution – no doubt as a product of the strong French-American links during the latter part of the 18th century. The French versions would probably be gilded or painted. From a famous set – probably of 12 armchairs originally – they were once owned by the family of Alexander Hamilton. They are almost certainly by the Philadelphian cabinet-maker, Adam Hains, and were made between 1793 and 1797. Other chairs from the set were probably made for use in The Vale, the country home designed by Samuel McIntire for Theodore Lyman of Boston: they are now on view in that house. Other chairs bear Hains' own maker's label, and some of

95

94

97

96

the set may well have been used by George Washington in the Presidential Mansion in Philadelphia and are now in the White House.

96. A Pair of Ebonized and Gilded Sheraton Armchairs, c1798, and Preliminary Drawings

Although these chairs are not identical to the design which Thomas Sheraton has signed on the engraving (bottom left), the similarity is probably as great as with any chair. The back panels are caned rather than covered with fabric, and the pastoral panel (which genteelly reflects the aristocratic preoccupation with rustic, idealized life) differs from the drawings. However, the turned legs, rope-twist arms and carefully-drawn proportions are the same. Close examination of the engraving shows that the top of each of the legs is different, which reveals Sheraton's intention to provide a guide rather than designs to be copied; in his *Cabinet Dictionary* of 1803, he notes, 'It is very remarkable the difference of some chairs of precisely the same pattern, when executed by different chair-makers, arising chiefly from the want of taste concerning the beauty of an outline, of which we judge by the eye, more than the rigid rules of perspective.' The book plate shows his skill as a draughtsman, although he clearly did not underestimate the maker's art; which is perhaps why his name is synonymous with late Georgian taste today.

97. Two American Hepplewhite Chairs, c1790

The chair on the left is from Rhode Island, and the other from Salem, Massachusetts. The latter was probably made by Samuel McIntire, but their similarity shows how standardized furniture design had become by this date; it is likely that they were both inspired by Hepplewhite books or other similar publications. However, there are differences; the Salem chair is lighter and more elegant, with no stretchers and, arguably, a finer back with more pleasing design. Both are good chairs of carved mahogany, typical of the Federal period, which corresponded to English Regency.

1800
TO
1900

Elizabeth of Bavaria's bed-chamber depicted in a watercolour, c1840. The hangings and the proportions of the room are grand enough, but the actual furnishing of the room reflect the mid-19th century taste for informality and comfort. The simple, clean lines of the chairs and other furniture shows that the so-called Biedermeier style, a more homely and comfortable derivative of the French Empire style, was not just a middle-class phenomenon.

The early design years of the 19th century were dominated by classical themes. Throughout Europe and the newly-independent America, interest in the ancient worlds was stimulated by excavations in Greece and Italy, and by Napoleon's campaign in Egypt in the last years of the 18th century.

Restraints imposed by financial hardships, too, affected the furniture designs of the time. In France, Directoire furniture was pared down structurally. In England, the early years saw the development of space-saving functional furniture. In post-revolutionary America, a new style combining classical lines and decorative motifs with indigenous patriotic designs developed a style that expressed the new America's pride in itself.

The Industrial Revolution had dramatic and immense effects on craftsmanship and design. New devices and gadgets had already crept into the designs of Thomas Sheraton by the end of the 18th century, as can be seen in his *Cabinet-Maker and Upholsterer's Drawing Book*, published between 1791 and 1794. But it was the influence of commercial manufacture which changed the face of design in England particularly, spreading throughout the rest of Europe.

Regency furniture in England took it name from the political Regency of the Prince of Wales from 1811–1820. Grecian influence in particular was fashionable (the 'Klismos' chair, which can be seen in London's Victoria & Albert Museum, was built from original drawings of ancient Greek seating), and much of the early work from this period was well proportioned and executed. However, in the main, mass-production had a negative influence on fine craftsmanship as mechanized furniture manufacture increased to satisfy the demands of England's growing population. Comfort became a prime feature, assisted by the cheaper production of upholstered fabrics. Much of the design between the 1830s and 1890s was based on revivals of earlier styles, including Chippendale, Louis XVI and particularly lighter Rococo, which all finally contributed to an amorphous, often bulbous, look which could be loosely called Victorian.

There were, however, several designer-craftsmen who were working against the current manufacturing trend, one of whom was William Morris. His company Morris & Co was to lead the way for the Arts & Crafts movement by employing contemporary artists such as Dante Gabriel Rossetti and Ford Madox Brown to design everyday furniture which was then handmade. Wider influences were looked for, and the new interest in Japan in the mid century caused Japanese art to be applied to their designs. Ernest Gimson and the Cotswold school similarly concentrated on cottage furniture, and through using the trade exhibitions around Europe, these socially-minded craftsmen re-established the concepts of hand-crafted furniture which were to influence the work of Scandinavian and German designers at the start of the 20th century.

Napoleonic France saw a decline of refinement in chair design from the time of the Empire (1800–1814) onwards. Imperial Rome was a key influence in Napoleon's reign, and Empire furniture was more for display than function – chairs were rigid and uncomfortable, becoming larger, deeper and more cubic, suggesting substance and grandeur – from the 1830s onwards, the effects of the Industrial Age crept in. As in England, a growing middle-class population provided an expanding market for furniture of all types, and machinery allowed the manufacture of far cheaper chairs. Revivals of Gothic, Renaissance, heavy Rococo Louis XV and XVI styles followed. Even though talented cabinet-makers were still at work, craftsmanship declined, and most new chair designs borrowed much from earlier times: deep, buttoned and tasselled chairs were rife, as were heavily upholstered pouffes and stools. One exception to this, however, was in the work of the Austrian Thonet brothers. Their new techniques for bending wood allowed them to manufacture one of the most popular chairs of all time – the Bentwood chair.

Elsewhere in Europe, Empire furniture had its influence, but the revivals seen in France and England – and especially Gothic, Renaissance and Rococo – were also prevalent. Influences spread faster thanks to the trend for international trade fairs, but national tastes continued to stamp revival furniture with individual marks; Italian decorative pictorial marquetry, for example, was copied by the English firm of Gillow.

America's Federal period also relied on classical influence, and the work of Duncan Phyfe, a cabinet-maker from New York, showed this at its best. Napoleon's Empire style soon reached America where it merged with native designs and styles. One notable exception to design trends was Shaker furniture, which retained simplicity and functionality. American chairs of the Victorian period retained influence from Empire styles, but a curious mixture of manufactured and handmade components of pieces lost much of the original refinement of earlier revivals. The interest towards the end of the century in Middle Ages and Renaissance work led to a revival of craftsmanship and a move away from mass-production.

1800-1900

98. A Pair of Regency Black Lacquer and Gilt Armchairs, *c*1800

This combination of black lacquer and gilt epitomizes Regency taste. Technically, the Regency period did not begin until 1811, but the term is used to describe furniture made between 1800 and 1820. The frame of these chairs is beech which has been ebonized to resemble oriental lacquer, although the manner in which the gilt is used is not at all to Eastern taste. The turned legs of gentle sabre form, and the scrolling horizontal arms, give a substantial, almost cubic, effect which characterizes armchairs of this period. The lion paw arm-supports and gilded acanthus scroll at the front of the arm are a simplified version of the exotic high-Regency style to come. These are, in fact, George III chairs made particularly attractive by the pictorial panels which form the back. These are painted in the *grisaille* palette (in tones of grey and black) which was first used to depict classical scenes on enamel and pottery in the late Middle Ages; typically revised and adapted, it works well here. The cane seats, covered with squab cushion, are broadened to accommodate the fashionable Beau Brummel coats of the period.

99. Two American Federal Dining Chairs, *c*1800

Whereas in England, furniture styles progressed smoothly through designers (Thomas Chippendale, then Robert Adam and the broadening influences of Thomas Sheraton, Hepplewhite and other pattern book designers), in America, the Revolution, which ended in 1783, caused major upheaval and a virtual end of new furniture imports until 1790. This limited the natural flowering of the Adam style, and many Federal chairs are based directly on, or closely inspired by, patterns from Sheraton and Hepplewhite, although the combination of decorative features is often unusual. The backs of these chairs, for example, are fundamentally simple square grids which have been embellished by vaguely Gothic panels and central satinwood inlaid panels. At a time when variations on established designs were the order of the day, any originality is greatly to be applauded. The chairs are almost certainly from New York, and are branded 'Anderson' beneath.

100. Two American Sheraton Chairs, *c*1805

American Regency at its best, these chairs are by a great chairmaker of the period, Duncan Phyfe, who worked in New York. The design is bold – drawn from 18th-century styles – yet innovative, combining turned columns, sabre legs and reeded rails on ormolu claw feet. The multiple, parallel carved lines give an almost Expressionist look to this sculptural furniture.

101. American Federal Chairs, *c*1805

These chairs (three of six) from the American Federal Period draws on various English prototypes and moulds them together into a unique American blend. The backs are shield or escutcheon-shaped, a design favoured by George Hepplewhite in his posthumous Pattern Book of the 1780s, while the inlay of husks and fan shapes is reminiscent of English Sheraton style as illustrated in Thomas Sheraton's Pattern Book. The tapered inlaid legs are also characteristic of English furniture from the turn of the century, although here it is mainly the use of inlay which gives the American flavour. The backs are unusual, with vertical, slender splats, and so is the position of the fan motif. English chairs would be more likely to be inlaid on the fronts of the legs; by English standards, these are a little top-heavy. They are the epitome of Federal elegance, the American equivalent of Regency.

102. Two American Sheraton Side Chairs, *c*1810

These chairs, with their extraordinary half-animal front legs are also possibly by Duncan Phyfe of New York. They epitomize American furniture of the time, very good quality English design with highly individual variations.

99

98

101

102

100

103. A Pair of Regency Simulated Rosewood Window Seats, c1805

By the beginning of the 19th century, chairs were sufficiently common to make stools redundant as seating in fashionable circles. This pair, however, are clearly fashionable stools and are very well built. They would probably have been placed beneath characteristically long, light, Georgian windows of the time. They have the typical Regency combination of dark wood and brightly-gilded, carved details; even the stretcher, which is almost invisible here, is beautifully finished. It is interesting that these are simulated, rather than solid, rosewood, which underlines the Regency approach that appearance was all, and fundamentals were less important. These stools are simply painted with a rosewood grain, a technique which was developed to a fine art, and it is often difficult to differentiate from the real thing. These stools also show the continuing presence of the X-frame from mediaeval times.

104. A Tahitian Wood Stool, c1800

If you were a member of the Iri or Nohara tribes, you may well have rested on one of these. It is, in fact, a rare example, as it is over a yard (3ft/1m) wide and carved from a single piece of breadfruit wood; this would have denoted the high status of its occupant. Primitive art, mainly Pacific and particularly African art, was extremely fashionable at the end of the 19th century, receiving greater exposure than before due to the French African colonies.

In the early 20th century, several painters, such as Pablo Picasso and Georges Braque, utilized primitive vigour as a source of inspiration, and so did Eileen Gray in her furniture for Madame Lévy's Paris apartment. Pierre Le Grain designed a variety of stools in both wood finish and sophisticated lacquer, such as the *Siège Curule*.

105. Two Silver-Mounted Anglo-Indian Chairs in Regency Style

These rather striking and elaborate chairs in Regency style show many signs of their Regency ancestors: the sabre legs, the reeded seat rail, and the rounded back with some organic decoration. It was not uncommon, as we have seen, for non-European craftsmen of the 17th and 18th centuries to produce copies either from a drawing, or from an actual European original; the effect was often charming although sometimes, as in this case, rather bizarre. The British severity of line is swamped here by the elaborately tooled and

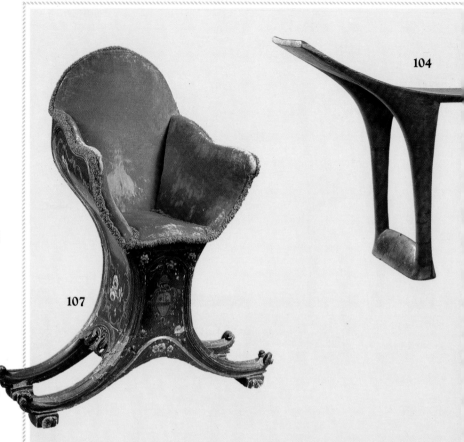

104

107

103

106

105

continuously decorated, thin-gauged Indian silver, and the chairs are not altogether successful. All these elements make these chairs extremely hard to date. Colonial pieces sometimes worked very well however, and often gave rise to a native export industry, such as the ivory artifacts of India and southern China. Although the English market does not always appreciate these hybrid pieces, the European Middle Eastern markets are often keen to acquire such goods.

106. A Regency Mahogany Bench, c1810

This is one of a pair of benches from Callaly Castle in Northumberland recently sold on the premises; the high price they reached is an indication of the taste of the 1980s. They are remarkable high Regency, a combination of organic forms (the back in the form of double eagles and the feathered paw feet on which the bench stands) and architectural ones (the rectangular seat with its reeded decoration and rectangular panels on the front). Also thrown in for good measure is a circular frame on the back, hung by ribbons, which was perhaps intended as a surround for a coat-of-arms, and a pair of battle-axes crossed in vaguely Imperial style. This is not so much a bench to sit on as a celebration of Regency quality and panache.

107. An Italian Gondola or Carriage Chair, c1800

This delightful Italian curiosity is more notable for its elegance than its practicality. As can be seen, it would not be very comfortable and was more of a ceremonial chair to be seen in rather than a chair to be sat on. Even its function is not clear, although it has been suggested that the outswept legs are especially broadened to sit on the edge of a gondola. It is known that these were certainly used in carriages of the time, perhaps in the same manner as a sedan chair. The decoration is principally rococo, flowering gilt all-encompassed by an asymmetric border; it shows how much more pervasive that highly decorative style was in Europe than in England.

108. A Regency Mahogany and Ormolu Armchair, *c*1810

This chair is very much in the manner of George Smith who published his book, *A Collection of Designs for Household Furniture*, in 1808. Curiously, on the underneath of one of the rails is written the name Smith, but while it is tempting to assume this was written by the man himself, there is no proof for this. All of Smith's favourite elements are there – the sabre legs, the scrolling arms and back, the generally cubic proportions (giving a massive look), and the dazzling contrast of gilded bronze on dark mahogany. This comes from the period when ormolu manufacture was at its height; on elaborate French furniture at the time, the gilded mounts chiselled by the *ciseleurs* often cost twice as much as the cabinet work itself. In England, Matthew Boulton founded his firm in the 18th century, which employed literally hundreds of craftsmen producing everything from solid silver to ormolu mounts for candle vases and furniture. There is little to surpass the quality of ormolu from this period.

109. A Regency Windsor Armchair, *c*1810

This is an excellent example of the traditional Windsor armchair form embellished with classic, crisp, elegant Regency decoration. All the uprights have finely-spaced spiral turning, the rails at the back and the splat have architectural decoration and fluting, and even the ordinary spindles have collars. Although the Windsor is thought of as being a country chair, it would have been expensive to buy new, and would generally have been found in a library or well-to-do home.

110. A Pair of Brass Inlaid Rosewood Dining Chairs, *c*1800

These chairs come from a set of eight chairs, comprised of six single chairs and two carvers. Made of rosewood with brass marquetry, they are absolutely typical of the good-quality functional Regency furniture which was produced by many makers of the time, few of whom stamped their chairs or recorded their names. These two show many Regency features – the sabre legs, the bowed seat rails which are caned to take squab cushions, and the lines of brass inlay along the rails and legs. The inlaid panels are an English version of a Middle-Eastern or Arabesque design indicating a subdued interest in the exotic, and the back stretchers too, with their cross design and central anthemion, demonstrate a classic motif.

Sets such as these frequently appear in the salerooms today, often in excellent condition in spite of having been used on a regular basis; a little of the brass inlay may have lifted from the wood, but this can be easily remedied. As rosewood became scarcer, these chairs were often produced in simulated rosewood, which was more economical although equally attractive, and this popular style was consistently produced over an extended period.

111. A Pair of Regency Giltwood Armchairs, *c*1810

Compared with some Regency chairs, these armchairs in the style of Morel and Seddon are relatively restrained and owe much to the styles of the late 18th century. While their form is Regency in weight and bulk, they are almost cubic (being wide and deep-seated) and give a strong horizontal impression with their use of large, flat planes. Beneath the gilt they are carved with typical Regency motifs such as the feathering on the side and back and the bulbous architectural decorations on the front legs. Large, generous and comfortable-looking armchairs, they perhaps lack the organic forms and exotic references used in high Regency style.

George Seddon (1727–1801) became master of the Joiners Company in 1795, 'a large fashionable firm employing about 400 journeymen, carvers, gilders, metalworkers and joiners'. Representing mainstream English taste rather than the avant-garde, the company was known to have enormous stocks of furniture, and was popular and flourishing into the 19th century.

108

109

110

111

112. A Regency Green Painted and Parcel Gilt Bergère, c1810

This splendid chair is one of a pair from the collection of the late author, Dame Rebecca West, and bears all the hallmarks of lively and exuberant Regency design and colour schemes. It is very much in the spirit of George Smith and his designs published as *A Collection of Designs for Household Furniture* in 1808. True to the Regency spirit, it is a medley of features and styles, and the gilt lion masks on lion-foot supports typify the fashionable trend of sculptural and organic forms. The broad seat rail gives a monumental air, and the long curving back relieves the otherwise bulky feel. While it is lighter than many armchairs of the period, it nevertheless gives a substantial impression, retaining the roughly cubic proportion which lend it such confidence and presence.

113. A Regency Mahogany Sidechair, c1815

The most unusual pattern on the back of this chair actually incorporates a handle as an original fitment; the back itself is very small, encompassing the central anthemion with concave curves, and standing on a stout seat and legs. Here we can clearly see the influence of European styles; the decoration is limited in order to emphasize the flat planes of wood, and the outline, which in this case is unusual, is stressed more than the applied decoration. This chair came from Great Tew Park, in Oxfordshire, and is related to styles in Napoleonic France, and to the continental Biedermeier style, which has clear, simple lines.

114. An Oak and Holly Window Seat, c1815

At first sight, this seat by George Bullock does not appear to be a piece of revolutionary design, but in fact this is the beginning of a revival, inspired perhaps by a reaction against the elaborate designs of Thomas Hope & George Smith. Note the date, 1815, and the woods, oak and holly – both are British. Nor is the decoration typically Regency (no eagle's heads, lions' paws or trophies of war such as spears or helmets), there is no ormolu, and the legs are primarily turned horizontally rather than fluted vertically.

This piece and its pair were invoiced in 1817 as '2 oak window-seats inlaid French stuf'd and covered with green twilled calico welted with yellow velvet £23 2/-', and come from the library of Great Tew Park. The

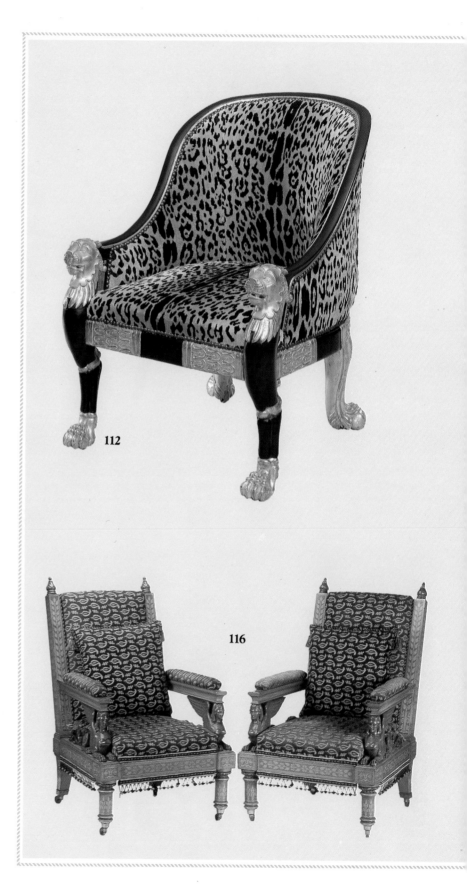

112

116

115

113

114

house was owned by Matthew Boulton, famous for his manufacture of Watt's steam engine and for his high-quality metal work in the late 18th century. The house is particularly interesting because it has remained virtually untouched from the time it was bought in 1815. The Boulton heirs were unwilling to modernize anything from the decorations to the electricity; consequently, much of the furniture mentioned on the original 42-page bill from Bullock to Boulton, dated 1817, remains. The library itself was designed by a Gloucester architect in the early 1830s, and is a fine example of the Gothic revival.

115. An Oak and Holly Sidechair, c1840

This side chair, executed by G J Morant, is also in oak and holly and probably dates from the 1840s. This is much more pronounced Gothic revival; the tapestry is probably original, with a Gothic design diluted only by a few central flowers, the back is a Gothic arch with carving above and the legs are turned in a vaguely columnar form.

116. A Pair of Early Victorian Armchairs, c1840

This pair of early Victorian chairs, again probably from the early 1840s, show an even more pronounced debt to Bullock. Also by G J Morant, they too use oak and holly, but the style of decoration is becoming much more Arts & Crafts, British woods with simple, unfussy British designs. The curious sphinx arm-supports are a retrospective Regency feature, and demonstrate how blurred changes in furniture styles can be. It would not be difficult to imagine that Morant's furniture, or the request for it, was inspired by the earlier, and therefore revolutionary, work of Bullock, who can be seen as a prophet of the Arts & Crafts movement to come.

117. A George IV 'Gothic' Window Seat, c1828

This is one of 28 oak window seats delivered to Windsor Castle in 1828 by Morel & Seddon, a leading firm of cabinet makers at the time. They were designed by Augustus Welby Pugin (1812–1852), who was the architect of the House of Commons and a major figure in 19th-century Gothic revival, a style which pervaded the second quarter of the century. Many of his chairs are in natural oak, and are almost invariably carved with the Gothic arch and a variety of tracery decoration. Colouring, another feature of Gothic revival, appears either in the painting of the furniture or the elaborate, sometimes garish, designs on the upholstery. Gothic is constantly revived in the history of applied art, whether by Walpole in the 18th century or by Pugin in the 19th century. The 19th century revival was partly underpinned by the ideas of the pre-Raphaelite brotherhood who felt the true nature of man, and therefore his art, had been reduced by the Renaissance; they logically therefore looked back to before the Renaissance, to the Gothic era.
Gothic was a very popular decorative scheme, used by architects such as Salvi to ornament the interiors and exteriors of buildings. Indeed, the style was so pervasive that it was popular well into the 20th century; the last great Gothic revival complex is the Wills Building in the heart of Bristol University. Finished in the 1920s, it looks like a ruined cathedral from the outside and a Victorian public school from within.

118. A William IV Throne, c1835

This William IV throne is exactly the kind of absurdly grand chair sometimes used to bolster a rather humble position. This throne has almost every Gothic motif, the arch, the quatrelobe circles beneath the arm, the mask heads, and the crested backs. It is not very much like a Gothic throne but it is wonderful nonsense.

119. A Pair of Rosewood Chairs, c1825

Gothic design extended to all types of buildings and furniture, including this pair of rosewood chairs. They are thought to have been supplied by Morel & Seddon, a name as much associated with cabinet making of this period as Pugin was with architecture and design. The proportions are cubic, with some upstanding Regency spirit fighting back, which was still the dominant style. The arm supports are fluted, with organic gilded carving below; the rails have typical Gothic

arch panels; and the legs resemble the windows of Gothic churches. In all, a move away from elegant Regency and towards chunky Victoriana.

120. A George IV Painted Bergère, c1830

In this George IV painted Bergère we can see that the Gothic style was not the only one to be revived as Regency declines. The decorative rosettes on the front rails of this chair are in fact the Tudor Rose, and the unusual, swirling, conical legs also emulate the Tudor period. The Tudor Dynasty reigned throughout the 16th century in England (from Henry VII to Elizabeth I) and ended in 1603. The architectural designs of Elizabeth I's reign had as much impact on styles of the 19th and 20th centuries than perhaps even Gothic; while the Gothic style is reflected in noble houses and late Victorian workers' estates, Elizabethan and pseudo-Tudor development influenced everything from Liberty's current building in Regent Street, London, a symbol of the Arts & Crafts Movement, to vast estates of commercially-built houses in the south of England. Tudor revival furniture tends to be grouped with Gothic, but it is an important bridge to the Jacobean revival of 17th-century pierced and carved work.

117

119

118

120

121. A George IV or William IV Mahogany Armchair, c1830

It is difficult to precisely date this chair for it has many late Georgian characteristics. It is heavy, and is probably late Georgian or even from the 1830s. The upper half and splat are still reasonably elegant with scrolling arms on lion paw supports; it is certainly of Regency proportions, broad with a deep seat. But the front of this chair is almost grotesquely heavy with thick melon flutes and a pseudo-architectural scroll on the top of the legs. This could well have been the armchair to a suite of chairs and shows clearly how quality continues from the Georgian period throughout the 19th century, and how the large wooden armchair was a key piece in the Victorian move towards comfort.

122. 19th Century Giltwood Rococo Revival Chairs, c1830

These two chairs are from a set of 12 from Inveraray Castle, the home of the Dukes of Argyll – the suite was reupholstered in 1871 when the 9th Duke married one of Queen Victoria's daughters. Should the Royal family, on seeing the asymmetric forms, deep carving and c-scrolls on these chairs have thought to themselves, 'What an excellent rococo suite,' they would have been both right and wrong. Although these chairs have all the characteristics of those from the 1740s and 1750s, these are in fact rococo revival. After the exotic Regency period – itself often a revival of earlier forms – chair-making generally moved to reviving earlier styles, one of these being rococo. So what is the difference between genuine and revival rococo? Sometimes nothing, although the average rococo revival chair is probably a little heavier in design, perhaps more excessively ornamented, and sometimes slightly different in quality though not necessarily inferior. In practice, it is very difficult to see the difference on two chairs of the same design without physically turning them upside-down and looking at the quality of the wood they are made of. If it is an original, the construction of the frame and the preparation of the timbers is by 18th-century methods, which include hand-sawn rails, peg joints and properly aged wood. The 19th-century chairmaker would have more sophisticated machines at his disposal, and might well have produced a better quality product with less human irregularity. Although he would have copied directly from an 18th-century chair or pattern, his spirit would have been influenced by his own recent history (presumably heavy Regency), whereas the 18th-century craftsman may have felt something new, French and adventurous was being created.

123. A 'Georgian' Revival Mahogany Armchair, c1850

This unusual English armchair is a magnificent but heavy example of baroque run amok. It is a curious combination of decorative motifs, mostly bird-like. The straight lines of the upholstery indicate 1740 or 1750, but the arm supports (apparently cockerels' heads) are curiously carved at the front with classical floral swags. The broad seat rail has a running architectural design above a gadrooned edge, and the broad cabriole front legs have eagle heads on the top flanking a cabochon beneath the shell, all standing on feathered ball and claw feet. The carving is deep and of very good quality, but slightly incongruous. The curious back leg is clearly a later replacement, presumably of an early cabriole.

It is in fact a 19th-century revival, and a very good 'repro' at that. In spite of its oddities, it is a wonderful, and slightly mad-looking, chair.

124. A Shaker Rocking Chair, c1840

This chair is typical of the light, strong chairs produced by the Shakers in the area around New Lebanon, in the United States during the second half of the last century. The slat back, the mushroom finials on the arm ends, and the conical finials on the back are common to that area, although the plaited seat and the rocker form are general to Shaker chairs from their communities in New England and the Mid-West.

The Shaker sect spread to America from mid-18th century England in 1774 and flourished in the early 19th century. Their beliefs in the simple life, common property and self sufficiency determined the style of country furniture which developed in their closed communities, and was marketed (by catalogue) from the 1870s onwards. Their belief that 'utility is beauty' now seems familiar, perhaps because it was echoed by the values of the European Arts & Crafts movement of the 1870s; the latter produced similarly retrospective, or traditional, shapes with rustic grace. The earlier the chair, the better the quality, often made with posts of naturally-seasoned maple, fruitwoods or pine. The early examples were frequently dark red, painted, or stained in pale colours; toward the end of the century, however, their individuality declined and stains were used to simulate conventional hardwoods. The Shaker movement has declined in the 20th century, although two communities do exist today and are living museums of Shaker craftsmanship.

124

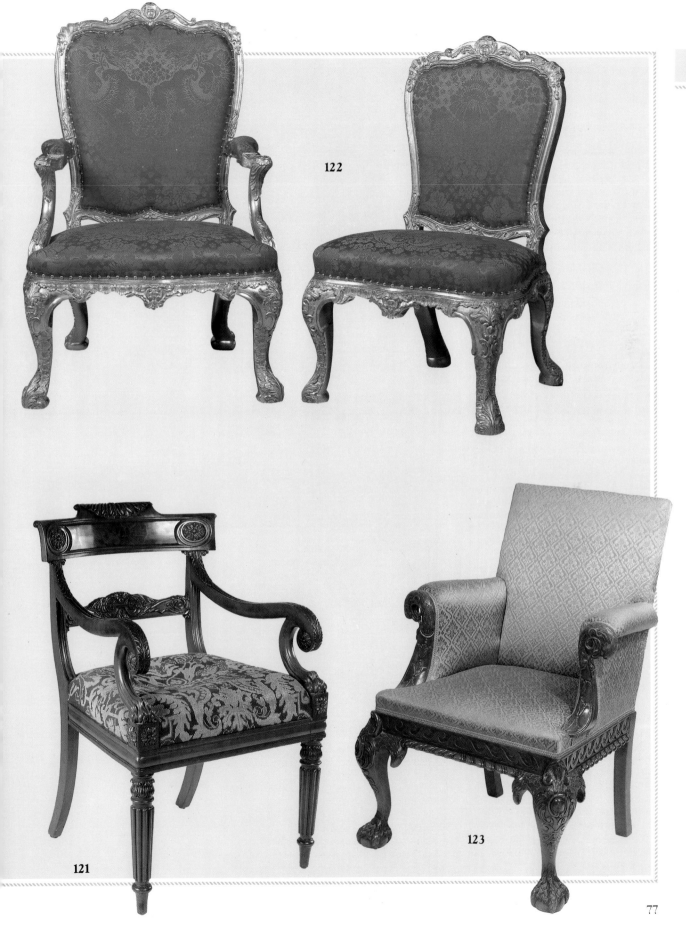

122

121

123

125. An English Satinwood Explorer's Chair, c1840

This delightful Victorian eccentricity is beautifully made of solid satinwood with brass and steel fittings. The maker's plaque is inscribed 'J Alderman Inventor Pattentee & Manufacturer, 16 Soho Square, London'. The extended handles, which are manufactured like the handles of surgical instruments of the period, were presumably for unhappy natives to carry the optimistic explorer through the relevant jungle. I have been assured that it also works well on the ground floor of a very well-known London furniture shop, given the right cooperation.

126. Two Chairs from a Suite of Spanish Furniture, c1840

We have seen how furniture in England and France lost its way in the 19th century after the tremendous creative surge of the first two decades. In Spain, the period of greatest affluence and Imperial expansionism was earlier, during the 17th and 18th centuries, and by 1800 it was in decline. This decline had a profound effect on the applied arts in Spain which tended to be dominated by the styles before 1750, especially baroque.

These chairs are a curious combination of the elaborate decoration associated with Italy and Spain, and the sculptural techniques of Andrea Brustolon and Antonio Corradini, 18th-century chair makers and sculptors, who had a lesser influence in England. The legs are astonishing rococo scrolls, upholstered in the characteristically Spanish painted leather often associated with Toledo. The overall effect is bizarre, although not altogether dissimilar to Antonio Gaudi's work of the late 19th century. Although much later, his work was also strongly influenced by Spanish tradition. One can see how the backs of these chairs are influenced by Imperial motifs similar to Regency and Empire, but the combination is pure fantasy.

127. Three Louis Philippe Giltwood Stools, c1840

Although French furniture became primarily revivalist in the mid 19th century, there were, as in England, occasional original and elegant creations such as these rope-twist stools associated with the work of Fournier. They bear little relation to anything that came before, apart perhaps from some elaborations of the rococo period, and are an amusing pun, reminiscent of the rustic furniture carved for The Great Exhibition of 1851 by Collinson from solid wood, which was intended to simulate natural tree branches with accompanying foliage. Here the result is elegant, French and amusing.

125

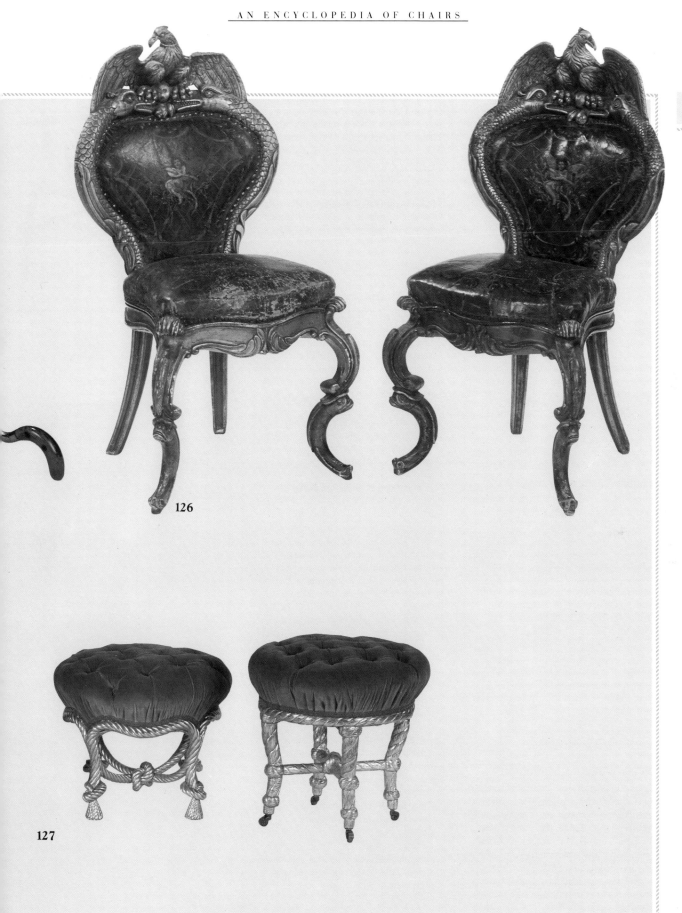

126

127

1800-1900

128. A Pair of Louis Philippe Boulle Armchairs, c1840

Louis Philippe reigned from 1830–1848, a period which roughly corresponded with a period of lack of direction in English furniture making; generally, English designers imitated earlier styles, such as Gothic and Jacobean. This particular pair of armchairs is very loosely based on the Louis XIV style, and in the manner of André Charles Boulle (1642–1732). He was a most celebrated *ébéniste* (cabinet maker) of the late 17th century and specialized in (and gave his name to), the technique of inlaying tortoise-shell with brass, or vice versa, for furniture which usually had elaborate ormolu mounts, like these chairs. Here, the high rounded backs and low seats are almost a caricature of the original styles, although the workmanship is still of good quality. European chairs and furniture have always tended to more elaborate decoration, and in France Boulle, as an elaborate style, continued well into the 20th century alongside Art Nouveau, as did Sheraton in England.

129. A Suite of Chinese Miniature Bamboo Furniture, c1850

This suite, measuring less than 1ft/30cms at its highest, was perhaps made as a toy for a child. It includes all the basic pieces of Chinese furniture: the altar table, which has miniature enamelled vessels on it, and is flanked by two large armchairs; a painting table in front (painting was a major Chinese scholastic pastime), flanked by a pair of slightly smaller chairs; and a side table for each one, with stretchers forming a 'cracked' pattern, emulating a desirable 'cracked' glaze on Chinese porcelain. The arrangement of pieces is formalized in this pattern for ceremonial purposes. It is interesting to see how real Chinese furniture relates to Chinese Chippendale; note particularly the aprons of these tables compared with 18th-century European fretwork.

130. A Windsor Chair, c1850

This good, if slightly late, example of an old friend, the Windsor Chair, perhaps represents the final stage in its development. Like most earlier models, the back is of yew and the seat of elm. The yoke, which forms the top of the back and the central splats, is fairly standard. It is interesting how the rest of the chair has been adapted to include the very Victorian habit of turning. Not only are the turned legs robust, but the central hoop which forms the arms is also on turned spindles,

giving a sturdy and pleasing effect. The good colour of the wood and overall good condition makes this stout chair a worthy offspring of its British Windsor extended family: contrast this chair with its 18th-century predecessors, or the American Windsor. There is today a Windsor chair industry based in High Wycombe, traditionally founded because of a nearby supply of suitable forest. The modern versions are generally beech, which rarely achieves the fresh quality or mellow colour typical of earlier types.

131. A Morris & Co Adjustable Armchair, c1865

This homely chair by Phillip Webb was based on the sketch of an actual chair found in a Sussex carpenter's workshop. When William Morris, filled with pious enthusiasm, founded his influential Arts & Crafts factory in 1861, he engaged a number of important artists such as the painters Rossetti and Ford Maddox Brown. In practice, Phillip Webb, an architect, was the source of many of the earlier designs, such as this chair, until Georges Jacques succeeded him from 1890 onwards.

The principles of the Arts & Crafts Movement suggested a return to earlier methods of handmade production by people in small communities using good British materials; good functional furniture would be made to fill the homes of the populace at a popular price. The firm operated from 1861 to 1940 and did in general conform to the principles which William Morris had originally set out, 'to execute work in a thoroughly artistic and inexpensive manner'. Inevitably, ideals gave way to practicality and Morris found himself later with a distinction between necessary, 'work-a-day' furniture and 'state' furniture. One could be forgiven for summarizing their production by saying the 'work-a-day' furniture was plain and the 'state' furniture was expensive, elaborate and impractical.

At a time when Victorian elaboration was the norm, Morris & Co made an important contribution, especially in designing fabrics, producing wallpapers, stained glass and tapestries. Their overall interior designs, still on display in the Victoria & Albert Museum, London, represent the more acceptable face of Victorian design. Perhaps his greatest contribution was reviving the notion of the artist-designer, which had a major effect on furniture making during the 20th century and provided a link between the Victorians and Art Nouveau.

130

129

80

128

1800-1900

131

132. A European Throne Chair, c1880

This astonishing creation is almost neo-baroque in style but is loosely based on Regency ideas. It has a wide repertoire of classical motifs – a sphinx, urn and anthemion borders; the elaborate upholstery continues the decoration in what is almost a *trompe l'oeil* visual illusion. The key to its date are the grotesquely large scrolling legs, and general lack of proportion; it does not quite have the Regency crispness and is probably mid-European.

133. An 'Egyptian' Mahogany Armchair, c1880

This extraordinary chair has been inconclusively attributed to a design by Christopher Dresser (1834–1904), an important influence on design in England in the second half of the 19th century. He was more of a scientist than an artist, at a time when the two were not so mutually exclusive as they are today. He worked as a Professor of Botany for some years, and then as a professional designer, notably of domestic metalware such as the functional kettles and pottery of the Arts & Crafts Movement. One of his main influences was Japan, where he spent some time. He later worked as the editor of the *Furniture Gazette* in which he published his famous, anonymous credo contending that function and purpose, along with economy and proportion, should dominate ornamentation. As with many great theorists, the results were sometimes very successful but often were not: that is the case here. This armchair looks expensive, uncomfortable, probably delicate and perhaps unhealthy. It is, however, a vehicle for delightfully anglicized Egyptian motifs and is great fun, a consideration which Dresser did not include in his credo.

134. The 'Thebes' Stool by Liberty & Co, c1884

If the East India Company in the 17th century was one of the first importers of Oriental goods and furniture on a commercial basis, and Liberty's was probably one of the last to do so before the exotic appeal wore off. In addition to stocking Far Eastern goods, Liberty became renowned as an outlet for Arts & Crafts products, and for near-eastern artefacts which the company itself distributed all over Europe. It gave its name to the Italian version of Art Nouveau, 'Style Liberty'.

135

132

133

134

Although Liberty commissioned well-known designers, most of its stock was sold simply under the name of Liberty. This stool – a relatively early piece of Liberty furniture – was made of rosewood and mahogany inlaid and decorated with ivory, and has a leather seat. There are great similarities to a stool found in the tomb of the Egyptian Pharoah Tutankhamun; which suggests that Liberty had taken an authentic Middle-Eastern pattern, and designed and manufactured a good quality, well-marketed product from it. By the 1890s Liberty had its own workshop, which also made Tudor revival products by well-known craftsmen.

135. An Armchair by Antonio Gaudí, c1885

Antonio Gaudí (1852–1926) was primarily an architect and is best known for his wonderfully eccentric Cathedral of the Sagrada Familia in Barcelona, Spain. He studied and worked in Barcelona, the cultural capital of Catalonia, all his life. He enjoyed the patronage of several of the great Catalan families and built excessive private houses and designed several public projects, including the park. His chairs, like his architecture, were highly original and draw on many sources, including the standard Art Nouveau motifs. Swirling lines fluidly describe volumes and planes in the French style of Emile Gallé and details echo the more traditional Spanish sources such as Gothic and baroque.

This armchair, a relatively conventional piece for a man of Gaudí's imagination, clearly leans heavily on the baroque, with its elaborate gilt scrolls which are not dissimilar to the furniture of the 1720s. Even the exaggerated studs on the upholstery have a slightly mediaeval look about them. Gaudi, like other architect-designers, created furniture to fit the style of his interiors, and this chair, designed for the Palacio Guell, Barcelona best fits a heavy baroque interior. As one might expect, his furniture is extremely avant garde, perhaps no coincidence in a city that is also the home of Salvador Dali, the great Surrealist painter and sculptor.

1800-1900

136. A Set of Oak Dining Chairs and a Dining Table by Ernest Gimson, c1890

This classic English design (136a) could date from the 1950s or 1960s, although its roots in fact lie in the Arts & Crafts Movement. The chairs are ultra-traditional; if they were executed in mahogany, the plain rectilinear backs, chamfered legs, and simple arms sloping to the seat might easily be from the 1780s, a provincial version of Georgian seat furniture. Their strength lies less in what they are than in how they were made. Ernest Gimson (1864–1919) was greatly influenced by William Morris, and although he always worked as an architect, he founded a furniture workshop in Gloucestershire around the turn of the century. Although he made little furniture himself, his workers used traditional British production methods without machines, with one man performing all the steps from start to finish. Gimson solidly refused to mechanize his production, believing that he was working to provide affordable furniture for the ordinary man. In practice, he probably made little profit and his furniture was too inefficiently produced to be enjoyed by any but the well-to-do. Much of his output was even more traditional than these chairs, an example being the 18th-century ladder-back cottage chairs associated with the skills of one of his workers, Edward Gardiner. Although his furniture could scarcely be called exciting, he must be admired for his integrity.

The strength of the original Gimson design can be seen in these two chairs (136b) from a suite by Peter Van Der Waals, the Dutch craftsman who worked for Gimson as chief cabinet-maker for Kenton & Co from 1901 to 1904. He produced these chairs in walnut and rosewood, again leaning towards the plain and severe lines of George III mahogany furniture. This too could easily have been the work of a provincial Georgian cabinet worker, whose simplicity no doubt touched the puritan soul of the Dutch. Gimson was a typical founder member of the English Cotswold School, designers and manufacturers working in that area combined by William Morris' ethics.

137. An Ebonized Sidechair, c1890

This unusual Arts & Crafts chair is attributed to John Moyr Smith but shows similarities to the designs of the revolutionary architect and designer Edward Godwin. Although chairs and furniture of this period are often well documented and can often be attributed to a specific designer in many cases, the generic term 'Arts & Crafts' sometimes sums up all that can be said about them. This chair is an interesting amalgam of ideas: it is somewhat like the work of Carlo Bugatti, and even shows some Regency tendencies such as the animal front legs and hooves, or the simple gilt design on the black background. Godwin was one of the first to fully translate Japanese designs for English manufacture, and in spite of the turned stretchers and homely English look there is an austerity here which shows oriental influence.

138. A Secessionist Walnut Chair, c1895

There is a restful simplicity about this chair. It seems to fall exactly between the influence of organic, sinuous, floral Art Nouveau, and the harsh, straight lines associated with the Vienna Secession. It was designed by Joseph Olbrich (1867–1908), a founder-member of the Secession who designed the Secession Building in 1898. At the invitation of the Grand Duke of Hesse, he moved to Darmstadt to found the artists colony there, both literally – in the design of the buildings – and also through his own ideological influence. He died there at the age of 41 after a prolific career; his furniture was mostly for the houses he built, although perhaps because of his early departure from Vienna, it has a timeless, universally applicable restraint compared to the creation of his fellow Secessionists Josef Hoffmann, Otto Wagner and Joseph Urban.

136b

138

137

136a

1800-1900

139. American Art Nouveau Chairs, *c*1900

These are truly transitional chairs; a combination of swirling forms and outlines of Art Nouveau, heavily decorated rails not dissimilar to those of the baroque revival, and a massive frame, very wide and low, a little like Regency chairs. They are by Solomon Carpen Bros of Chicago, US, and were made around the turn of the century.

Art Nouveau was perhaps more of a European style, because of the turn of the century Paris exhibition. In Europe the organic forms and motifs of Art Nouveau had quickly taken root everywhere from the furniture to the architecture, whether by Antonio Gaudí in Spain or Victor Horta in Belgium. The United States, particularly the provincial states, focused more on geometric architectural style than difficult-to-produce, curvaceous, European forms.

140. Two Sidechairs by Carlo Bugatti, *c*1900

Carlo Bugatti's chairs and designs for interiors are wonderfully eccentric and difficult to categorize. They draw heavily on the Near East for inspiration (Syria and Egypt particularly) in their use of applied and worked metals, such as the copper on the left-hand chair, and the extensive inlay of many different materials – here, pewter, ivory and other woods. He had no fear of mixing different materials and methods; the seats on these chairs are made of vellum (fine skin normally used for writing), and hung with tassels.

Vellum became one of his trademarks, as did the circle or half-finished circle, and the chunky geometric look. At the 1902 Turin Exhibition in Italy, for example, the wood of some of his furniture was covered entirely in vellum, and sporadically decorated with abstract and naturalistic designs such as insects and birds. Bugatti originally trained as an architect before opening his first furniture workshop and outlet in Milan in the 1880s. He also produced silver jewellery and other goods. He is perhaps most famous for his sons, Rembrandt – who became best known for his impressionistic animal bronzes – and Ettore, the sports car designer.

140

139

141. An Italian Art Nouveau Suite, c1900

This combination of elegance and function typifies the work of Ernesto Basile and Vittorio Ducrot. It was designed by Basile, who was primarily an architect but in 1898 became chief designer for the Ducrot's firm, a sizeable interior design workshop in Palermo, Sicily. They designed extensively in the 'Liberty' style (the Italian version of Art Nouveau which took its name from Liberty's in London) as well as in more organic styles. They completed some prestigious projects and exhibited at Italian Fairs in the early years of the century, but overall, the firm's direction was more commercial, producing good quality, stylish furniture such as that of the Grand Hotel, Palermo, for general use.

142. An Art Nouveau Walnut Armchair, c1900

This classic Art Nouveau chair is attributed to, or designed by, Georges de Feure. It evokes the fluid, curvilinear, organic style of the turn of the century. It is not outrageous; indeed, it has the same fundamental structure as a restrained Louis XVI tub chair, and is a reminder that most Art Nouveau furniture was relatively normal and not necessarily innovative or bizarre. On this chair, the uprights are traced with lines in relief and have a suspiciously organic look, confirmed by the elaborate swirling pattern on the seat rail which joins the gently curving legs. De Feure was in fact capable of much more elaborate creations than this, and contributed to Samuel Bing's *Pavillon de l'Art Nouveau* at the Paris 1900 exhibition. He was not a furniture designer by trade, being primarily a painter and engraver; his designs for silver, ceramics and traditionally-influenced graphics won popularity and public acclaim in several European countries.

143. A Chair by Charles Rennie Mackintosh, c1897

Charles Rennie Mackintosh designed for the improbable setting of a Glasgow Tea Room (Miss Cranston's Tea Room in Argyle Street) a chair (143a) which is perhaps more famous than any other, and which was exhibited at the Vienna Secession in 1900. Mackintosh's personal philosophy was that chairs should fit their setting – in this case, to create an intimate space in which to converse over tea – and to phrase the room in the most appropriate terms. Mackintosh was a revolutionary figure with tremendous impact, particularly on the Vienna Secession (he spent some time in Vienna), and also on Frank Lloyd Wright who developed in a parallel fashion in the United States.

As an object, this chair is a highly original composition of geometric form which describes space in a very architectural way. Its proportions are perhaps closest to a throne, being over 4ft/122cms high, and with a broad splat at the back which gives it a massive appearance.

The same design was also executed in upholstered painted wood, for another Mackintosh Interior (143b). Mackintosh liberated design through his close links abroad, even though his personal architectural output was low. He is best remembered for the Glasgow School of Art building, which exhibits his changes in style (from organic to geometric) as building progressed, and as a source of inspiration for a group of radical Scottish architects called 'The Four'. After his stirring career, he gave up architecture in middle age and went to France to paint.

144. A French Pearwood Chair by Hector Guimard, c1900

Guimard was an influential Art Nouveau architect who introduced the work of Victor Horta to Paris, and this French chair has all the curvaceous lines and elegance of French Art Nouveau, a style which involved interior fittings and decorations, as well as the exteriors. He is famous for the characteristically sinuous entrances to the Paris metro.

This chair shows many hallmarks of the Nancy school of design, in northern France. Although the glass maker Emile Gallé was the first President of the 'Ecole de Nancy', founded in 1901 as a type of industrial design cooperative, it had several other important members who also made important contributions. Louis Majorelle, Eugène Vallin, Gallé and also the Frères Daum, produced both furniture and glassware. Their chairs are particularly noted for their classically Art Nouveau qualities of organic swirling loops with reeded detailing and stylized flowers. Gallé claimed that the new style referred only to decoration, and that his structures were fundamentally traditional. Nancy became almost a marketing operation, but the strength of image created constraints which the French designers Suë et Mare rejected in their manifesto.

143a

144

143b

142

141

1900
TO
1988

An early 20th century interior design by the Finnish architect Eliel Saarinen. Saarinen's design shows strong influence from contemporary designers of the Vienna Secession like Hoffman and Moser, and his high-backed tub chairs echo the work of the Scottish architect Charles Rennie Mackintosh. The 20th century saw the first real rethinking in chair design since the 17th century and Eliel Saarinen's son, Eero, was one of the most important chair designers of the mid-20th century, pioneering the use of materials like plywood, glass fibre and plastic for mass production.

Throughout the 19th century, communications had improved, and the large international fairs of Paris, London, Philadelphia and Chicago had meant more sharing of ideas was possible than ever before. New materials, such as plastics, plywood and tubular metal, were introduced, and two main directions appeared: the Arts & Crafts movement's interest in line was developed in England and America, then elsewhere in Europe there was a move towards the decorative swirls, based on floral and organic forms, of Art Nouveau. The successors of these two were encompassed in the eclectic Art Deco era which peaked in 1925.

The work of the Art Nouveau artists was ornamental and highly expressive. Of pure form based on function, quality of material and workmanship, emphasizing social purpose by economy of production'. In retrospect, the glittering movement that produced pieces from individuals such as Emile Gallé and Charles Rennie Mackintosh showed enormous individual talent.

The more dominant trend in 20th-century design was that of the northern Europeans – the Scandinavians and Germans. One of the first to design attractive functional furniture for mass-production was the German architect, Richard Riemershchmid. His chairs were specifically designed for factory production, and consisted of several elements produced separately and then nailed together. This radical approach was mirrored by the Dutchman Gerrit Rietveld, a founder member of the De Stilj group of artist-designers. Their belief in using only primary colours and rectangular forms, and a commitment to the Machine Age, led to their continuing influence on modern chair construction through simplicity and lightness.

In 1903, the Vienna Secession, under the leadership of architect Josef Hoffmann, transformed itself into the Wiener Werkstätte (Vienna Workshop) whose studios manufactured Werkstatte's typical grid-like designs, mainly in black and white. In Scotland, Charles Rennie Mackintosh abandoned Art Nouveau curves and founded the Glasgow School which concentrated on line and geometric patterns. In Germany, the Bauhaus movement blossomed within a decade into a force that still influences furniture design today. Originally headed by Walter Gropius, who later moved to the United States, it encouraged its participants to seek new design answers to problems of material and function. This is exemplified in the work of Marcel Breuer which also shows the link between the Dutch De Stilj movement and the Bauhaus. Brauer's early experimentation with tubular chrome chairs led to countless derivations; Mies van der Rohe, for example, exhibited his Barcelona chair at the German Pavillion of the Paris *Exposition Internationale des Arts Décoratifs et Industriels Modernes* of 1925, the showcase of the Art Deco movement.

Art Deco threw up a host of talented and innovative designers in all spheres of the arts, including chair design. Working in France in the 1920s, Le Corbusier redefined furniture into three categories – chairs, tables, and shelves – and designed standard pieces for the interiors of his buildings accordingly. Although individual, his chairs show the desire for 'anonymous' design that pervades the second half of 20th century – equipment, rather than art. In the United States, Frank Lloyd Wright was also designing pieces for his own interiors, and the chairs he designed for his own house were clearly indebted to the Arts & Crafts movement. In England, designers were less innovative, tending to react to these movements as they arrived from Europe and the United States, although the design firm of the PEL (Practical Equipment Limited) were soon using metal tube and plywood in their chair designs.

The suppression of artistic expression in Germany of the 1930s changed this northern European domination. Both between and after the wars, Dutch craftsmen continued to work in the handmade vein to great effect, but mass-production supremacy moved overseas. In Finland, Alvar Aalto – one of the most prolific designers of modern times – played an interesting role, falling between the traditional craft approach of Scandinavia and the new forms developing in central Europe. His bentwood forms echo those of the Thonet brothers in 19th-century France, but belong unmistakably to the 20th century.

After the Second World War, American design flourished with an influx of talented craftsmen and designers such as Walter Gropius and Eliel Saarinen before and during the two World Wars. Saarinen's son, Eero, and Charles Eames worked with plastics, fibreglass, and moulds which have been imitated and adapted worldwide since that time.

Plastic has become a commonplace material for furniture in the second half of this century. Its effects on design were crucial, moving the emphasis away from decoration and back to fluidity of line. More recent developments show a growing division between designer chairs for the collector and the development of the mass market.

145. Oak Spindle Chairs by Frank Lloyd Wright, c1901

These chairs, typical of Wright's furniture, clearly owe a great debt to Mackintosh. Wright first designed similar chairs for his own dining room, which was very geometric, stark and fundamentally based on a grid. Linked with developments in the Glasgow School and in the Vienna Secession, this chair is tall and linear (about 5ft/1m 52cms high) and its undecorated austerity is akin to Japanese design.

Frank Lloyd Wright (1867–1959), born in the United States a year before Charles Rennie Mackintosh was born in Scotland, had a profound influence on American design, living through all the major styles from the Arts & Crafts Movement through to the 1950s. He subscribed to the holistic approach to design, which suggested that furniture in the many houses he designed should reflect the shape and spirit of the space which it occupied. He practised this to an almost excessive degree, producing a sparse style that architects and designers loved, but which was not particularly practical. Although Wright designed some economy furniture for ordinary use, it is obvious that this chair uses a vast amount of timber, would be expensive to produce and, as can be seen, when gathered around a table would effortlessly congest any normal-size environment. In spite of this, Frank Lloyd Wright was certainly one of the United States' most important 20th-century architect-designers, not least for his early treatment of the relationship between furniture and its surroundings.

146. An Oak Sidechair by Frank Lloyd Wright, c1920

This chair (146a) in Wright's familiar materials, oak and leather, was designed for the Imperial Hotel in Tokyo, Japan. Again, it is minimalist and geometric in line, based on the hexagon and the octagon, and is another example of Wright's desire to fit the movable furniture to the spirit of the immovable space in which it is contained. He insisted on designing everything for the hotel, including fabric and carpets. The structure itself was built of concrete and so survived the disastrous earthquakes of the 20s, before falling prey to property developers in 1968.

Frank Lloyd Wright's influence can be seen on furniture executed by George M Neidecken, c1910, for the E P Irving House in Decatur, Illinois, US (146b and 146c).

147

149c

145b

145a

149b

149a

148

146b

146a

146c

147. An Office Chair by Frank Lloyd Wright, c1904

This early example of adjustable office furniture was made for the completely fire-proof building of brown-painted steel of the Larkin Company in Buffalo, New York. It is a strange combination of Secessionist design, with its geometric lines and grid decoration, and a functional modernity.

148. An American Sidechair by Frank Lloyd Wright, c1950

Designed for the Trier House, this chair combines Wright's main ideals; that furniture should be sympathetic to its surroundings, and that it should be accessible to all, the plywood construction being cheap to manufacture.

149. Chairs by Josef Hoffmann, c1905

This is a good example of Josef Hoffmann's bentwood designs, executed by the specialist factory of Kohn & Kohn (149a). Hoffmann was an influential architect, closely associated with the Vienna Secession and later to be a founder of the *Wiener Werkstätte* (literally, the Vienna Workshop) in 1903. Although he was radical in his designs, being much influenced by Mackintosh, he was also highly respected, and taught at the Vienna School of Arts & Crafts for over 30 years.

One of the signatures of his chair designs are the curious lobes or spheres which support the joints on the front legs. The backs of these chairs are a pastiche of a Sheraton tea tray, decorated with an inlaid fan in the centre. Hoffmann also designed furniture with sharp, geometric motifs, often decorated with grid-like patterns, and sometimes studded leather with brass caps to the legs.

The other two chairs pictured here (149b) are from a set of six, and show the emphasis placed on simplicity and respect for tradition. Although many of his clients were extremely affluent bourgeois Austrians, Hoffmann also published furniture designs under the title *Simple Furniture*, which he considered to be an aspect of good design.

Hoffmann was a prolific designer of chairs, some of which are faithfully reproduced today by Franz Wittmann. This, the *Biach* chair (149c) shows Hoffmann's command of the bentwood medium, as produced by his own factory. Characteristically using geometric shapes, simple straight lines, and spherical supports at the joints through which screws join seat to leg, the design was light, economical to produce, yet sturdy and stylish.

1900-1988

This dining chair c1908, the *Armlöffel* or Arm Spoon (149d), clearly shows the original spirit of the Secession: austere and angular, it is decorated with the grid pattern only, one of Hoffmann's strongest trademarks. He included this chair in several of the interiors he designed, the only departure from sharp, straight lines being the spoon-like arm rests which give the chair its name.

This later chair (149e) was designed for the Haus Koller in 1911, and shows the impact of the Art Deco movement on Hoffmann's designs. The Haus Koller was a more sumptuous and luxurious enterprise than his turn-of-the-century interiors and this chair shows nothing of the straight, geometric lines or purist look seen earlier. Its chic, sculptural forms are soft and welcoming, altogether more organic with the edges highlighted with another of Hoffmann's trademarks: the tape with alternating black and white design. The long, straight, upright curves show how Hoffmann was not insensitive to the Art Deco style of the 1930s; this could almost be by the famous Deco *ensemblier* (interior designer) Emile-Jacques Ruhlmann.

This *Kubus* armchair (149f), designed in 1910, could easily be the product of Bauhaus in 1930. Its name derives from the cubes which make up the upholstery, although in fact every part of the chair is a pure geometric shape; even the castors are hemispheres. The resemblance to Bauhaus comes in its large, flat planes which are not dissimilar to the work of Walter Gropius or even some of Marcel Breuer's early works, such as his easy chair of 1923. The proportions are similar to those of a Regency chair.

150. An American Art Nouveau Armchair by Greene & Greene, c1908

Without knowing its origin, first sight of this chair suggests many sources. Its form is that of the caqueteuse, with the high back and splayed arms of the 16th century; the starkness and decoration suggests something of Japan; and the splat and emphasis on the grain of the wood could almost be Morris or Mackintosh. It is in fact American, designed by Greene & Greene for the Blacker House, and like all their chairs, was commissioned by clients for their architectural projects.

The brothers worked mostly in California, and greatly admired the work of Gustav Stickley, using some of his furniture in their first houses. Interestingly, they originally attended the St Louis Manual Training High School, which, as its name suggests, laid great emphasis on manual skills; perhaps this gave them their love for wood, which was

149d

149e

149f

150

extensively worked to reveal the grain rather than simply varnished. Both were trained as architects, and though Henry continued, Charles gave up architecture to explore his ideas that art consisted in making the everyday beautiful, and that form would emerge from the medium itself. Of the two brothers, Charles probably designed most of the furniture; he visited England in 1901, and had the same admiration for Japanese taste as the English Arts & Crafts makers. Greene & Greene were enthusiastically received in Europe, and were perhaps the most English of the American Arts & Crafts designers.

151. Norwegian Painted Chairs by Gerhard Munthe, c1911

A crucial aspect of the tremendous changes in the perception of design represented by Art Nouveau (and Art Deco) was the wide scope for *individual* development that they afforded: despite the attempts by many scholars and critics to categorize Art Nouveau works as, say, 'organic' or 'linear'.

The delightful fantasy chairs by the Norwegian Munthe are a perfect example. These are simply a virtuoso indulgence of decoration; the sculptural, carved mask heads clearly come from Scandinavian folkloric tradition, and likewise the interlacing strap-work has a Gaelic look to it. The naïvely carved scene on the back panel doubtless depicts a fairy-tale episode. The chair absorbs many different styles from arabesque to Regency, all converted into this burst of colour. Here, the new stylistic freedom is productive rather than limiting.

151

1900-1988

152. Chairs by Gerrit Rietveld, c1917

Gerrit Rietveld (1888–1964) was a natural designer, trained in cabinet-making, jewellery, and then finally architecture. This chair (152a) demonstrates immediately that something dramatic has happened in the development of furniture. 1917 marked the transition between the organic, curving Art Nouveau style and crisp, chic Art Deco. Here there are suddenly straight lines and complex shapes formed out of the most simple techniques coupled with striking colours. It can be argued that Rietveld certainly marked, if not began, a revolution which in a sense continues today.

The dramatic interplay of straight lines to form patterns was not a wholly new idea – in the 1860s Godwin, greatly inspired by oriental design, produced geometric household furniture. Similarly, Mackintosh, Lloyd Wright and the Viennese designers such as Hoffmann used lines to produce shape. Here, the lines produce form by enclosing space; the structure has very simple components, and the chair's colour is reminiscent of the geometric painting of Mondrian, whose famous squares of colour are concerned with proportion. The link with art was no coincidence since Rietveld formally joined the Dutch De Stijl movement around this time, a movement which promoted simple form and primary colours. This chair was a complete original, unlike anything made before, and represented an absolute departure from traditional structure. It removed the remaining design rules.

Rietveld's second great chair (152b) was the Berlin Chair, designed for the Dutch Pavilion at the Berlin Exhibition in 1923. In some ways, it is an even more exaggerated demonstration of belief in the principles of De Stijl; it is much simpler, and uses only tones of black and white. Although much less famous, it is in some ways more pleasing and is truly sculptural in the way it encloses space and portrays mass. It is free from the excesses of previous decorative styles, such as Gaudí's neo-baroque or even earlier 18th-century designs; in this chair, everything is totally functional. If compared with the Schroder House in Utrecht, which Rietveld designed in 1924, it can be seen that both have the same stark, functional construction, creating form by placing similarly-shaped slabs in different planes.

To show his command of diverse materials, in 1927 Rietveld designed the Beugel Fauteuil (152c); it may look like the Red-Blue chair in plywood and tube, but in fact it takes its strength from all the integral triangles from which it is formed. Rietveld's chairs were never merely artworks. He founded his own

152e

152h

152b

152a

152g

152c

152f

152d

workshop and retailers in 1911; many of his original designs were produced by G A Van Der Groenekan, and this chair was mass-produced by Metz & Co in the late 1920s – such is the revival of interest in the De Stijl movement that recently even the paper bags designed by Metz & Co and printed labels used by Rietveld as a trademark on his Red-Blue chairs have become collectable items; some were recently auctioned in Amsterdam.

Rietveld's imagination was inexhaustible. He produced many single chairs, side chairs and low chairs, such as the Military chair (152d), 1923, an unapologetically functional object made of very simple joints and inexpensive materials which dismantles completely. The Piano chair (152e) was a rather more design-conscious piece of domestic furniture made of mahogany billets joined with wooden dowels, and with simple leather fabric. Clearly a continuation of the line construction of the Red-Blue chair, it has a dramatically different effect. Rietveld also produced chairs in other media (examples are rattan or wickerwork), some of which proved to be less successful. His zig-zag chair (152f) was another striking departure from tradition and he made the prototype himself in 1934. Later produced by Van Der Groenekan, it is of a design so simple that one wonders why it had never been done before; although the joints on the Z had to be extra strong, this was achieved by simply bolting the two parts around a dove-tailed joint. Typically, the materials were very simple and it could be produced cheaply, a continuing theme in his work. In 1934, he produced the Crate desk, a desk that could be made with no more material than would normally be used to make a packing case. In the same year Metz & Co produced the Crate chair in red spruce, a design which has been revived and is in production today.

Another of Rietveld's truly original ideas were the chairs sculpted from a single sheet of fabric, showing his concern for the method as well as the result of design. The Birza chair (152g), designed in 1927, was in theory cut from one piece of fibre which was then folded and fixed into a rigid shape. It was designed for the Birza Room, an interior which took the name of its patron, Dr W Birza. The overall effect shows similarities to the work of Frenchman Emile-Jacques Ruhlmann in the shape and the sabre`legs, and echoes the achievements of the Bauhaus and Scandinavian designers in plywood. Unhappily, technology had not quite caught up with Rietveld, and Van Der Groenekan allegedly refused to make others by the designer, because of the trouble he had had with the first. The same theme recurs in a remarkable aluminium chair (152h), designed

during the Second World War, made from a single piece of aluminium stamped with holes and held together with riveted buttresses. Although it looks like a space-age fantasy, to the designer it was an exercise in economy of material, combined with structural strength to give interesting form. He designed most of his chairs by actually emphasizing the material used rather than the original idea.

153. The Napoleon Chair by Edwin Lutyens, c1919

This unusual, asymmetric chair was designed by the famous architect Edwin Lutyens for his own use. It is called the Napoleon chair because he had seen a painting of Napoleon sitting on a similar piece of furniture. The piece has never been traced. Lutyens had a pair of these chairs built for his own fireside in Mansfield Street, London, appropriately a large house designed by Adam. He had such affection for them that he even had a pair made for the miniature library in Queen Mary's Doll's House, which he finished in 1924. This example is in fact c1988, since the design is being commercially reproduced by Lutyens' grand-daughter, and is based on the example in the Victoria & Albert Musuem, London. So, this is a 1980s revival of an Edwardian revival of a Napoleonic chair.

154. A Set of Chairs and a Games Table by Emile-Jacques Ruhlmann, c1920

If one thinks of Art Deco furniture as being chic, then Emile-Jacques Ruhlmann (1879–1933) is surely the most typical Deco designer. Even in his day he was hailed as the successor of the great 18th-century French cabinet-makers, and in the design of these chairs there are striking similarities. The elegant tapering legs with the brass caps, very characteristic of Ruhlmann's work, are similar to the stylized French and English chairs of 1800–1820. Although the upholstery here is fairly restrained, Ruhlmann often used exotic fabrics such as leopard skin with coloured woods and lacquering. After tentatively exhibiting his work before the First World War, he came to dominate French interior design in the 1920s. His devotion to the excesses and the virtues of elitism could not be further from the ideals of the English Arts & Crafts movement, or the soon-to-dominate German Bauhaus.

155b

154

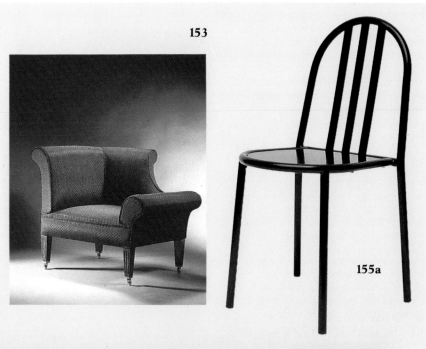

153

155a

155. A Dining Chair and an Armchair by Robert Mallet-Stevens, c1920

Robert Mallet-Stevens (1886–1945) was a French architect-designer, and most of his chairs were made to fit his interior schemes. They were primarily of tubular construction, placing great emphasis on simplicity and plain design which could be economically produced, rather as Hoffmann had done at the turn of the century. France, through the work of designers such as Emile-Jacques Ruhlmann, had formally led the way in design with high quality, sumptuous and expensive craftsmanship. Combatting the increasing competition from cheap and functional Dutch and German imports became one of Mallet-Stevens' concerns, and one which he championed as a member of the Establishment in the 1930s, moving his own design away from lush Deco style.

156. Lloyd Loom Chairs by W. Lusty & Sons, *c*1925

Although primarily thought of as being garden furniture, and advertised in 1922 as being 'ideal for the garden room or sun parlour', Lloyd loom furniture has achieved classic and popular status. It was born out of a mechanical innovation by Marshall B. Lloyd, a pram manufacturer from Menominee, Michigan. His wicker prams, highly fashionable with the Victorians, were made by weaving split-wood cane or rattan by hand, much as they had been since the 17th century. Traditionally, the warp was fixed to a frame and the weft inserted over and under alternately. After several attempts at mechanization, in 1917 Lloyd devised a machine which would weave fabric in a similar way, but at 30 times the speed.

The wicker that Lloyd wove was primarily fabric, but in England production was by W. Lusty & Sons of Ruskin Works, Bromley by Bow, London. The Lustys' version was described as having a 'heart of steel', an 18g steel wire in every upright wrapped in coiled paper. The manufacturing process was relatively complex. The new woven fibre was moulded around a frame, generally of beech but sometimes metal after 1956, and the parts were then joined together while the wicker was still soft. It was then sized and baked to make it rigid. Steam-cleaned in caustic soda, spray painted and baked again, this gave a smoothly-woven, evenly-painted look with a glossy finish. All Lusty Lloyd loom had a metal trade label and was stamped with the date and year of manufacture. There were literally dozens of different models. More flexible than wood, it was perhaps more like plastic than the original wicker. There were wing chairs, sidechairs, dining chairs, occasional tables, linen baskets and pedestal cupboards on anything from bracket feet to cabriole. The seats were of three grades, one stuffed with wire wool, another simply plywood, and for the greatest luxury rubberized foam on Hessian fully-sprung (on which I am now sitting as I type).

The early pieces were the most adventurous, with the designs coming from the United States, and at one time Lusty created a development department for innovation. A family partner tellingly observed that 'he got it all wrong. What it needed was a technician, not an artist. In the end everyone experimented with designs which had to be sculpted and sometimes a good one turned out.' While this philosophy was in sharp distinction to the ideas of other designers of the time, there is no doubt about the popularity of what it produced. In the firm's heyday, paint was mixed in quantities of 10,000 gallons a time. In an edition of *The Cabinet Maker*, 1930, the editor stated: 'Such perfection of weaving and comfortable springing is now found in this woven fibre furniture that it is in the most constant use in the most fashionable households, liners, cinemas, lounges and dance halls.' These enduring designs were competitively priced to allow use by all. Lusty Lloyd loom are shortly to recommence manufacture, a pointer to the quality of their original design.

157. An Asprey Dining Set, *c*1925

These throne-like Art Deco chairs were commissioned by an Indian Maharajah from Asprey of Bond Street, London, to accompany the glass-and-chrome illuminated dining table. The table is inlaid with panels by René Lalique of France, whose firm is best known for its decorative tableware, and art glass. Combining these delicate panels, depicting birds among foliage, with heavy square-sectioned legs, has a monumentally impressive effect. The chair is stylish and unique.

158. Art Deco Salon Suites, *c*1925

This suite (158a) was designed by Louis Süe and André Mare who in 1919 founded the Paris interior decorating firm, the Compagnie Des Arts Français which did much to popularize Art Deco. Their declared aim was to allow a cohesive style to develop without the suffocating singularity of Art Nouveau, in its French form dominated by waving organic stems and budding flowers. Süe et Mare were architect and painter respectively who combined with various other craftsmen working in fabric, wood and even glass, to produce some prestigious interiors. This suite was for the famous Exposition des Arts Décoratifs held in Paris in 1925. Although their work was prestigious and exclusive, they favoured the use of traditional skills and artists to create a more sober, though still sophisticated, look in the increasingly bizarre world of Paris in the 1920s.

The suite is based on a Louis Philippe prototype. Louis Philippe (basically French 1840s) drew heavily on the designs of the Louis XV and XVI periods a century before. If this suite was upholstered in traditional cloth and some of the sharp Art Deco corners were softened, it could be seen to be very much in an 18th-century style. The use of the Beauvais tapestry is itself retrospective, similar to the tapestry workshops set up by the Arts & Crafts movement in England at Windsor, to emulate the work of the Mortlake workshops of the 17th century. This suite in a style revived twice over still has an essence of Frenchness

157b

158b

157a

156

158a

about it, the product of a national concern for style which has developed its own identity over the centuries.

The second suite (158b) by Maurice Dufresne uses straight vertical lines contrasting with gentle horizontal curves, which are echoed in the seat rails and set off the tapestry; the result is not excessive, but still chic.

159. The Wassily Chair by Marcel Breuer, c1925

This chair, perhaps one of the most famous of all 20th-century designs, later took its name from the artist Wassilly Kandinsky for whose studio it was made at the Bauhaus. Breuer (1902–1981) left Hungary to study painting in Vienna and in 1924 took charge of the Bauhaus workshop concerned with interior design. He encouraged the students to produce in simple media, in keeping with the broad principles of originality and function. The stylish Wassily chair has been in continual production since 1925, and its historical importance in generating the designs of Mart Stam, and Mies van der Rohe is undeniable.

As political difficulties dogged the Bauhaus, Breuer moved to England where he helped the firm Isokon to develop designs using sculptured plywood, which again sparked off an entirely new generation of furniture. Remarkably, he was considered much more important as an architect and was invited by Walter Gropius, former head of the Bauhaus, to teach at Harvard University in the United States in 1921. He continued his impressive, celebrated career in the United States, and in the end, in spite of the grandeur of his buildings, it is his chairs which arguably have had the greatest impact.

160. The Transat Chair by Eileen Gray, c1927

Eileen Gray has become one of the best known individualists in 20th-century design, and this is perhaps her most famous chair, originally made for a house she built at Roque Brune in France, on Corbusier's recommendation. She was born in Ireland in 1879, trained at the Slade School of Art in London before 1900 and then became an apprentice at a lacquer workshop. She worked all over Europe during the next 30 years with many of the great names of the 20th century; as can be seen from this chair, she took elements from each. It is elegantly simple, punctuated with germanic brass fittings, has a French look, and yet leans toward Mies van

der Rohe. Like Frank Lloyd Wright, her long life saw many styles come and go, and her interior designs particularly survive them all.

161. Chairs by Mies van der Rohe, c1929

Ludwig Mies van der Rohe (1886–1969) was another architect-designer from the influential German Bauhaus of the late 1920s; his two main designs – the Barcelona (161a) and the M R (161b) chairs – had tremendous impact on subsequent 20th-century furniture. Mies van der Rohe was born the son of a German stone-cutter and was apprenticed to a furniture designer and architect, Peter Behrens. He started working for himself in 1912. The Barcelona chair takes its name from the Barcelona International Exhibition for which it was designed, with accompanying ottoman or footstool. Although swiftly conceived, the modernist German pavillon at the exhibition, with straight lines and minimal encumbrance, was a great success, as were the chairs, produced in Berlin and still made by Knoll International today.

Although a director of Bauhaus from 1930–1933, his furniture designs disregard economy and concentrate on opulence. The flattened steel frame of the Barcelona is in fact quite complex and relatively expensive to produce. He was most famous, however, for his furniture made from tubular steel, generally chromed and close to an original design by Mart Stam which consisted of a continual tube bent to form base, legs, seat and back. Mies van der Rohe was first to patent the idea, although he claimed that it worked on a different principle to Stam's original. This became the basis for the M R range, designed in 1931, with comfort depending on the springing in the tubular frame and the luxurious leather upholsteries. The simple appearance is deceptive; more for aesthetic reasons than structural ones – his famous maxim was that 'God is in the details' – the chair was very carefully designed to give this air of simplicity. Before the Second World War he fled from the Nazis to the United States, where he was for many years the director of the Illinois Institute, Chicago. Able to develop many of the ideas he had formed as a young man in Germany, he produced some dramatic works such as the Lake Shore Drive apartments in Chicago in the 1940s, and the Seagram Office building in the 1950s.

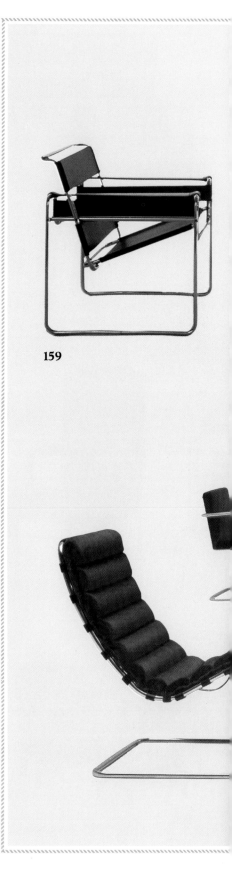

159

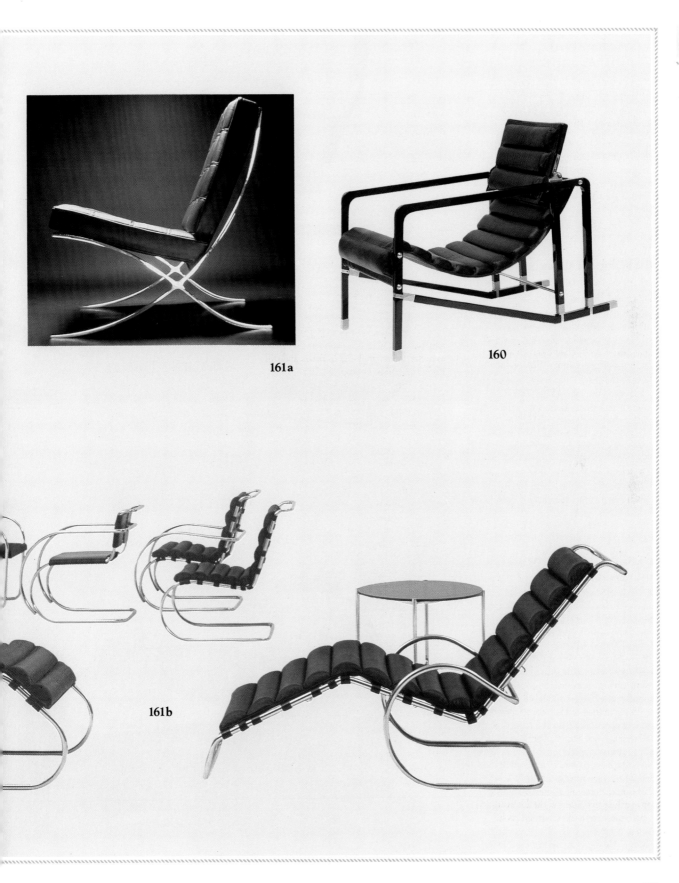

161a

160

161b

162. A French Chair by René Herbst, c1930

René Herbst (1891–1982) lived in Paris and produced a variety of minimalist designs, including a series of chairs based on chrome stretched with expandable elastic. This chair was one of a series, which included armchairs and chaises longues, with a classic simplicity and function. They are reproduced by Écart today. Herbst claimed that the two necessary conditions of modern art was the rejection of ornamentation, and purity of line. The result is French Bauhaus, with the addition of a little chic.

163. A Suite of Wrought-Iron Art Deco Furniture by Raymond Subes, c1935

If the straight lines and elongated forms of this suite clearly belong to the Art Deco movement, the style of the chairs perhaps best indicates its source – revivalist. If one were to change the proportions by flattening and widening the chairs, they would have an oval back, a broad seat, the gilt details and dignified drapes more familiar from the state chairs of the Napoleonic era. Even the marble table underlines the analysis; wrought-iron supports of a U-shape are not unfamiliar beneath the brightly patterned marble of Napoleonic console tables. The furniture certainly borders on the kitsch, and may be more at home in the wrought-iron tradition of Mediterranean furniture.

164. Chairs and Stool by Alvar Aalto, c1937

This chair (164a) is one of an original series of laminated wood furniture, the Scandinavian equivalent of Bauhaus tubular steel. Alvar Aalto (1898–1976) was a major Finnish architect of the Modernist movement, concerned not only with the spaces in the buildings in which people lived, but the furniture which occupied those spaces. His belief that the fitments should be as human as the people in them led him to reject metal in favour of organic, or natural, products. Aalto's early designs were exhibited at Helsinki in 1931 showing unusual shapes which were the results of his experiments with wood in the 1920s using some tubular support.

When designing the Paimio Sanatorium during the early 1930s, the first project that brought him international attention, he wanted to get away from tubular metal for the furniture. He therefore devised the Paimio chair on a laminated frame with a veneer seat

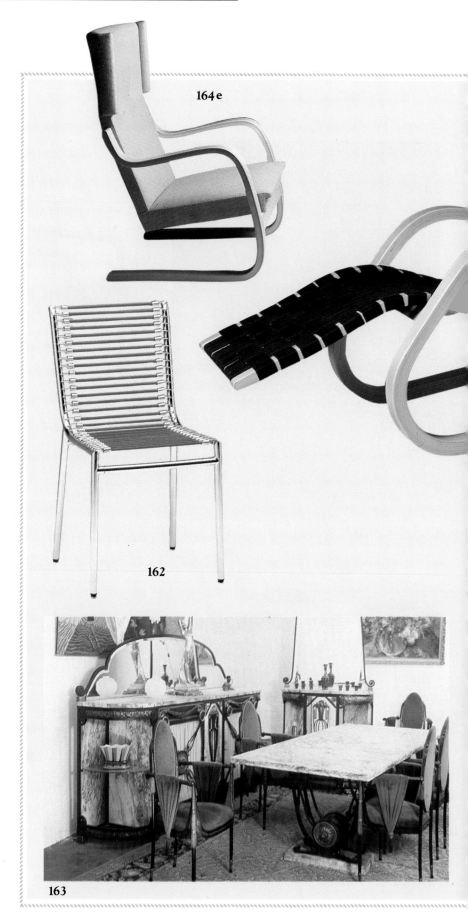

164e

162

163

164a

164d

164c

164b

(164b). Friendlier than other chairs, it also
has a delightfully bizarre shape, as unusual as
anything from the rest of Europe and self-
sprung on the natural flexibility of the wood.
The easy chair is covered with a lattice of
webbing, and when fully reclined resembles a
chaise longue. The design cleverly reduces the
need for complex techniques in production;
there are few corners to be joined or joints to
be made, the wood is virtually continuous and
the linear appearance pleasing. Aalto founded
a firm known as Artek which still produces his
furniture today. It is not all exotic; the
stacking stools designed around 1930 for the
Viipuri Library (164c) were simple, functional
and space-saving, an idea which he continued
with a similar chair of simpler design, without
the laminated springy legs made of several
leaves of wood (164d). By 1933, he had
designed a broad range of extremely variable
furniture including his high-backed armchair,
not dissimilar to a traditional 18th-century
English Wing Chair (164e).

Comparisons have been drawn between
Aalto's laminated birch furniture and moulded
plywood furniture produced in the 1930s by,
for example, Summers and Eames; the
fundamental difference is that Aalto makes
the structure work in the design, producing an
integrated whole which is also elegant. His
designs have a classic appeal which remains
popular today.

165. A Pair of Laminated Birch Sidechairs by Gerald Summers, c1938

With the influence of design exhibitions,
which were now plentiful in most European
capitals, and an influx of European designers
such as Marcel Breuer, the Modernist style
gradually filtered into England. Although this
ultra-modern furniture was associateed with
the design firm PEL (Practical Equipment
Limited, a branch of the artistic Isokon
Group), there were also self-styled craftsmen
working with the new techniques. Gerald
Summers, who designed for the firm Makers of
Simple Furniture, created some highly original
models. This elegant design is delightfully
simple and economical; it is simply a cut-out
of wood which is bent round and held together
by the seat rails, a little like folded paper. The
result is pleasing to look at as well as being
cheap and practical. The same principle was
used in his more famous plywood armchair,
which again was cut out of a single sheet of
material, the arms being bent upwards and the
legs being bent downwards. It is surprising
that such an innovative idea did not achieve
greater acclaim or commercial success.

166. An Italian Plywood Chair by Carlo Mollino, c1945

This unusual variant (166a) on the plywood
chair is by Carlo Mollino of the Milan School
of Designers; Milan had become an important
design centre between the two World Wars,
and home of the Triennale exhibitions.
Mollino is perhaps the best-known name from
this period. His most famous design is the
unusual reclining chair of 1949. The more
conventional chair is not dissimilar to the
work of Gerald Summers and has the
sophistication of being sprung by the
tensioning bars between the legs. It was
manufactured by Apelli and Varesio. The
Milan School's designs are exciting, especially
when compared with much of the post-war
British Utility furniture.

Most of Mollino's designs in plywood use
the natural tension of the bentwood in the
same way as Aalto and Summers: this
prototype (166b) is also moulded to give added
shape.

167. LCW ('Lounge Chair Wood') by Charles Eames, c1946

Charles Eames is perhaps the most famous of
modern chair designers, and is certainly the
most collected. He is rightly applauded for two
notable achievements: for using plywood
which could be permanently moulded in two
planes rather than in one, as Gerald Summers
and Alvar Aalto had done; and secondly, as a
designer of truly sculptural chairs, partially the
result of this technique of exploiting complete
freedom in three dimensions. The joy of really
pliable plywood was that the seat and back
could be moulded exactly to the human form,
dispensing with the need for upholstery. After
the Second World War there emerged a new
generation of chairs based on this principle,
partly devised in collaboration with Eero
Saarinen, using plywood glass fibre and then
plastic on a variety of supports. His designs
were recognized in the Second World War,
were exhibited in the Museum of Modern Art
in New York, and in 1948 won a prize in an
international competition for low cost
furniture design, appropriately combining
cheap and easy production with design
elegance.

168. An Oak Dining Suite by Gordon Russell, c1950

Immediate similarity can be seen between this
suite and the suite pictured earlier by Ernest
Gimson, and establishes Gordon Russell as
having inherited the best aspects of the 19th-
century Arts & Crafts movement, as seen in

166a

168

165

167

166b

the work of the so-called Cotswold School. Russell was slightly less anti-mechanist than Gimson; indeed, he became a specialist in industrial production and during the Second World War designed for the British 'Utility furniture' scheme, which concentrated Great Britain's resources on making only one type of furniture as cheaply as possible.

The design of these chairs is retrospective, and almost identical to English Farthingale armchairs of the mid-17th century. Similarly, the table is based on a heavy, rustic, distinctly non-technical design. The quality of the furniture is discreet but excellent. In *Design Magazine* in 1951, Russell wrote that the 'tradition of pioneering should prove to be a decisive influence when a survey of the situation in AD2051 comes to be written'. While this may be the case, it may be thanks to the innovative work of designers such as Race rather than to the retrospective work of Russell & Sons, Broadway, Worcestershire.

169. Chairs by Harry Bertoia, c1952

Although Harry Bertoia's most famous chair, the wire-grid backed dining chair, became a lasting image of the 1960s, it was in fact designed in the early 1950s. Bertoia was an immigrant from northern Italy, where he grew up surrounded by Milan School chairs which clearly influenced him greatly; in the United States, he became a metalworker and a student sculptor. He met Eero Saarinen and Florence Knoll, and worked for some years with Charles Eames who is now considered the most important 20th-century American designer. His work with Eames after the Second World War on plywood and metal designs clearly influenced his own development; in this range of wire-structured chairs, some of them support sculptured seats in manmade fibre reminiscent of Eames' work of this period. Bertoia described them as being 'mainly made of air, like sculpture. Space passes through them.' He spent much of his life working for Knoll International (who still produce the chairs shown), producing designs directly for their factory and also fulfilling architectural commissions of sculptural kinds. These amorphous shapes and bold colours have come to symbolise the United States' West Coast of the 1960s.

170. A Pair of Black Lacquer Chairs, c1952

These chairs by Isola and Gabetti, with their unusual stretchers joining the legs in an interesting (but uneconomical) way, have a sculptural quality not dissimilar to the works of Carlo Mollino. They share with his work the acceptance of a notion of upholstery versus structure, and achieve impact with their bright colours.

171. Chairs by Eero Saarinen, c1955

With the exception of tubular steel furniture and some bentwood designs, almost all the chairs in this book have four legs, which come independently from the seat. Saarinen said of his pedestal design that 'the underside of typical chairs and tables makes a confusing and restless world . . . I wanted to clear up the slum of legs'. It is hardly surprising that he worked closely with Charles Eames: the fruits of their partnership formed at the Cranbrook Academy of Art, Michigan, US, (of which Saarinen's father was director and architect) are easy to see in his soft-outlined, sculptural seats.

Saarinen was born in Finland in 1916 where his father was a major architect. He grew up, however, in Chicago where his father designed the 40 buildings of the Cranbrook Academy of Art in Michigan, and for one of which Eero designed the furniture. In 1940, he designed with Eames a range of furniture based on plywood shell which was featured in a competition for organic design in home furnishings, organized by New York's Museum of Modern Art. There is something very European about the outline of these pedestal chairs, a design which was also present in his collaboration with Eames and which perhaps goes back to his European origins, even though most of his life was spent in the United States. Like Harry Bertoia, his chairs have become one of the lasting images of the 1960s, the Tulip chair appearing in the first English Habitat catalogue of 1971.

170

171

169

172. The Coconut Chair by George Nelson, c1956

Although this chair appears to be soft and sculptural, it is in fact supported both by steel legs and by a metal shell which keeps the fabric upholstery in shape, hence the name Coconut. They were commercially produced by the Herman Miller Furniture Company. The chair shows the strong influence of Charles Eames and Eero Saarinen, paves the way for greater design freedom in the 1960s, and was exploited on a large scale by European designers. The metal shell eventually gave way to fibreglass and other modern materials, truly popularizing this style.

173. A Fibreglass Desk Chair by Jean Lele, c1969

Although this looks as dated now as it was outrageous at the time, it in fact represents a coming-together of three distinct trends. First, it owes a debt of origin to Charles Eames, Eero Saarinen and even Harry Bertoia who exploited and explored the use of new materials in a soft, sculptural way. Second, it fully exploits the possibility of fibreglass, its great strength and ease of construction, and creates an integral sculptural environment for the user – this idea was not a novelty, many people have sat at Victorian desks with folding bench seats – but what is new is the harmony of line in this extravagance. Third, it marks the outer boundary of the avant garde as allowed by the new materials (just as it could be said that the English Habitat designs of moulded-fibre furniture were the inner boundary). A brief look at the 1980s shows a regression from this degree of innovation, or at least a return to more traditional forms.

174. The First Habitat Range of Chairs, c1971

War-time shortages in Europe had seen a new generation of designers and therefore designs emerge. By the 1960s the main technological changes, the use of plastics and new materials, had given new freedom to structures, and designers such as Charles Eames or Vico Magistretti were not slow to exploit the possibilities. The 1960s also saw a marketing revolution as represented, if not begun, by Englishman Terence Conran with his Habitat shop. The notion of selling furniture in kit form to be assembled at home was not a new one; Gerrit Rietveld and Bauhaus designers had used this technique 50 years before with some success. Mass production was not new either; Giles Grendey and Thomas Chippendale, for example, employed vast workshops in the 18th century, and the

Thonets produced many millions of bentwood chairs in the 19th century. However, the Conran combination of high-volume production sold in kit form via catalogue soon became tremendously popular.

The first catalogue of 1971, from which these three illustrations are chosen, combined Habitat-designed wares with other designers' work including that of Eero Saarinen and Harry Bertoia. The mass production kept prices down, and imaginative room settings in the catalogue promoted the idea of more stylish households; easy access by post or by visiting the rapidly-growing chain of stores ensured Habitat's success. There is little in the first catalogue of enormous originality, as can be seen from this selection, centred on practical 1960s clean lines, with bright colours and some up-market modern furniture classics, including Conran's own design line. The Habitat range created a demand for bourgeois style which it then exploited with a chain of stores somehow very different from the traditional British quality stores, such as Heal's or Waring & Gillows. Interestingly, the largest single feature in the catalogue on chairs is taken up by photographs of Thonet's bentwood chair, 'no 14', designed in 1859.

175. Two Boxing Glove Chaises Longues by De Sede, c1978

These chairs, or arguably sofas, are nearly 3ft/91 cms high and 5ft/152 cms long, and are magnificent for their wit. It is surprising that such a delightful and sensuous form had not been thought of before. There is, however, more to it than mere novelty; it belongs to a branch of art which is the descendant of Surrealism, or even of visual illusions as enjoyed by baroque painters. In the 1930s, Dali thought that chairs were taken too seriously and devised one that constantly fell over and even spilt drinks! These chairs are not dangerously challenging or disturbing, and in this sense they are not surreal: they are a gentle joke at the expense of design pretension. They do not try to 'break the monopoly upon that which is real' (Ehrenzweig). After all, they really are quite comfortable to sit in, and 'comfortable' is not a word normally associated with Surrealism!

172

174c

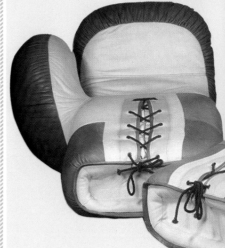

173

174b

174a

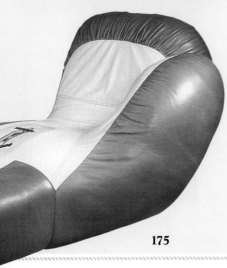

175

1900-1988

The following ten chairs (176–185) have been selected by the British Crafts Council as being of exceptional merit. They differ from most other contemporary chairs in that they are generally made in small numbers, in contrast to international firms. Each chair has been subject to rigorous examination by master craftsmen and is therefore fundamentally sound.

176. A Glass Chair by Danny Lane, 1980s

Pundits claim that Lane has already become a classic, the sort of comment one is bound to get when dealing with contemporary art. However, the chair is certainly dramatic. It is the sort of glistening apparition which the 17th or 18th centuries would have greatly appreciated. Glass chairs are extremely scarce, although some were produced in the 19th century in formal, throne-like, precisely-cut material. Made of dozens of individual slices of float glass which are held together by rods in columns, it is only just a practical chair, being extremely heavy and not very comfortable; and the accompanying chaise-longue is even worse. But it is exciting and amusing, epithets which could equally have been applied to elaborate rococo or more bizarre Regency designs. This chair has a sculptural quality of which Gaudi or even Bugatti would have been proud.

177. A Bench by Andrew Holmes

Initially, Andrew Holmes' furniture has a slightly off-beat 1960s look, perhaps because it is primarily made from materials from demolished houses. Holmes is a sculptor by training and views his furniture as functional – a popular 18th century notion – and indeed this bench shows similarities to Gothic box chairs, with the same homely air. He argues that muted colours are reassuring – a latter day Alvar Aalto?

178. A Steel-Framed Chair by Eric de Graaff

The first impression of this opportunely photographed chair is its emphasis on structure, underlined by the use of colour quite separate to the 'upholstery'. The sharp geometric lines forming squares and rectangles owe a clear debt to Gerrit Rietveld, also to Josef Hoffmann and the Vienna Secession, or even Charles Rennie Mackintosh. An appealing feature of this chair is the way the lines which form the frame not only support the body but also enclose and define space, which is in turn punctuated by the flat planes forming the seat and the back. It works well in that it is beautiful and reasonably comfortable.

179. A Chair by Fred Baier

Fred Baier produces furniture in a variety of styles, and recently completed a large commission with another graduate from the Royal College of Art, London, for a celebrated circular Art Deco mansion in Surrey, which included a circular double bed. Fitting the form of the furniture to the form of the house has echoes of Frank Lloyd Wright, although this particular chair in stained sycamore with leather and horse-hair upholstery has a quasi-Italian look about it, vaguely reminiscent of Carlo Mollino. Whether or not academic exposure to a history of style is always beneficial, Baier chairs are well-crafted, imaginative and generally sensible.

180. A Caterpillar Rocker by Jeremy Broun

This chair is visually stunning, a good combination of colour, structure and practicality. The frame is of stained birch plywood, the slats are red-black mahogany. It has the advantage of being a truly original idea: just as Saarinen and his pedestal chairs converted four chair legs into one, so this chair seems to be altering the design of the rocking chair. Not simply concentrating on structure and colour, it is fundamentally changing traditional designs in a move towards simplicity. Broun is first a craftsman, second a designer and this is perhaps the most avant garde of his work. He is quoted as saying he 'likes to take a risk with material' and to 'exploit its character'; it is an achievement to do this without losing direction.

178

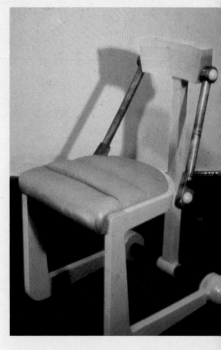

179

180

176

177

181. A Sidechair in Beech by Richard la Trobe Bateman

There is more than a hint of Gerrit Rietveld about these very straight lines, geommetric patterns and simple joints. Richard la Trobe Bateman considers that economy of means, clarity of technique and practicality are important principles, a view which Rietveld would no doubt have applauded. They are good-looking chairs made with interesting techniques, such as the splitting of green timber. They have been called Constructivist, which apparently means they show a serious concern for disciplined, logical form. However, they suffer perhaps from Rietveld's problem of beauty without comfort.

182. A Folding Chair by David Colwell

This is a true craft chair, based on a traditional design and executed in traditional fashion: the timber has been bent by steam while still green and then left to season. It was made in a workshop in Wales by a small team in the Morris-style Arts & Crafts fashion, and the X-frame is one of the earliest forms of European chair dating from the Middle Ages. It is appropriate that it should be revived in this more modern folding form.

183. A Set of Dining Chairs by Rodney Wales

These simple chairs are an interesting combination of many different styles. The caqueteuse, a 16th-century form, had a very slim back and a hemispherical seat like these, although here the backs have been stylized into almost Mackintosh proportions and have reminiscently square-silhouetted designs, not unlike Secession design. Wales has won awards for a combination of good design and potential for mass production. The simplicity of the chair suggests that the potential popularisation is great as it takes design away from the rarified elite and places it in the home.

184. A Chair in Cherry Wood by Rupert Williamson

One can instantly see from the complex structure of this chair that it requires cabinet-making skills worthy of any good 18th-century craftsman. There is much 18th century Chinese Chippendale chair in the design, although there is no carving (a practice which is almost defunct in modern design, presumably because of cost rather than taste). It has a great sculptural quality about it, the back forming a splendid almost Gothic arch

183

186

185

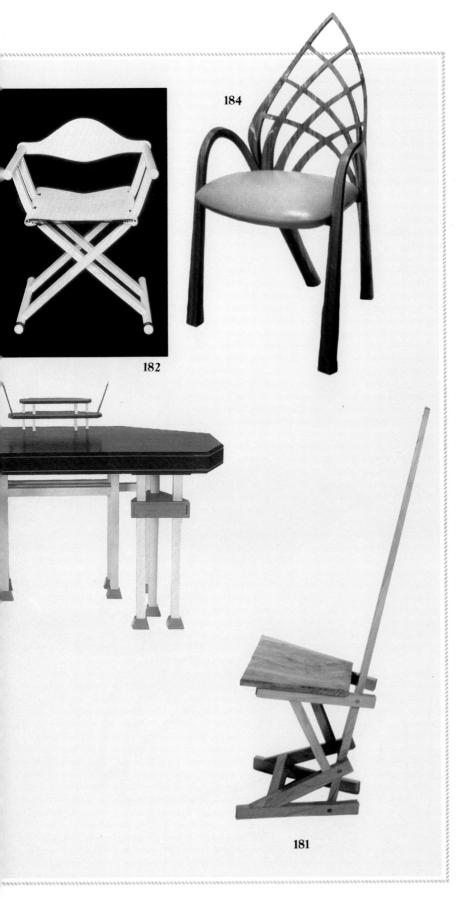

184

182

181

above a long sweeping down-turned arm, reminiscent of Hepplewhite. One of Williamson's chairs is in the Victoria & Albert Museum, London, which perhaps suggests that these are modern chairs for the antique lover.

185. A Chair by John Coleman

This elegant design by John Coleman has the regrettably rare quality of being the right shape for the body. This important criterion seems to have escaped the majority of chair designers from all periods. The angled back clearly gives plenty of lumbar support, allowing the lower back to curve in its natural direction – forwards rather than in an injury-prone backwards.

This chair has clean lines, and is practical. It is primarily of ash, and is made-to-order, reviving the close link between maker and customer which is often now long and strained. It is homely but not dull.

186. The Oil Rig Desk and Chair, by Stephen Owen

Salvador Dali, the Surrealist painter, claimed that chair design was taken far too seriously; Stephen Owen has effectively avoided that pitfall. This design based on an oil rig in Art Deco revival style utilises straight lines and geometric patterns to give it a lively effect which punctuated with the bright colours contrasting with the black. It is an amusing example of novelty furniture made acceptable by wit.

187. A Folding Chair by Phillippe Starcke

Phillippe Starcke is something of a 1980s cult designer with an impressive track record: he designed the French presidential apartment at the Elysée Palace, the night club *Les Bains Douches*, as well as several American hotel chains. The appealing thing about this chair is its simplicity, practicality, and elegance of line. It clearly looks back to PEL, or perhaps the Bauhaus and Gerrit Rietveld for its roots. It has the very real advantage of being practical for modern living and not expensive to produce.

188. 'Mister Bliss', a Chair by Phillippe Starcke

Characteristically linear, this is a surprisingly rare attempt to design a chair on which to kneel, a far healthier posture than sitting. It is extraordinary that new designs shows such little regard for comfort and health, preferring an impressive look. This chair is based on the principle of increasing the angle made by the body and legs to more than 90°, which allows the lower back to curve inwards in a natural way; most chairs have the opposite effect.

189. The Spaghetti Chair by Gian Dominico Belotti

Gian Dominico Belotti, born in 1922, is from the pre-Second World War generation of Italian designers. He originally studied sculpture and later followed an architectural training in Milan where he was more concerned with ideological considerations than commercial ones. This chair, designed in the late 1970s, showed an interest in materials and a simplicity belonging to the Marcel Breuer tradition, which continued after the Second World War.

190. A Chair by Carlo Forcolini, 'Signorina Chan'

This striking, contemporary chair contrasts the sculptural element of the triple-curving back with the linear element of the straight, stark tubular frames, and the two strong colours, contrasts which perhaps pervade the decade. It is no surprise that Forcolini was a pupil of Vico Magistretti; indeed they have worked closely together producing 1980s designs which tend toward richness and indulgence, far removed from the simplicity of the Minimalists.

187

188

189

190

191. 'Quarta', a Chair by Mario Botta

Mario Botta trained at the Milan School of Fine Arts in the early 1960s, did some practical work in the studio of Le Corbusier, and now works as an architect in Lugano, Italy. This chair, the fourth of an interesting series, combines linear elements (each surface being made of slats) in a sculptural way. Although the image is exciting, the planes formed are very hard. This would not perhaps win an award for comfort, but it has the visual impact which Italian design frequently does, and several of Botta's designs are in the study collection at the Museum of Modern Art in New York.

192. A Chair by Vico Magistretti

This is a classic Milanese chair, relying on simple elements and yet having a sculptural quality. Vico Magistretti graduated in 1945 and began to design in the period of post-war rehabilitation, following the original pioneers such as Terragni and Carlo Mollino, whose work this in some ways resembles. Magistretti exhibited and won awards at numerous Triennales, and his work in the Milan movement, which has become an originator of international style, can be found not only in the first Habitat Catalogue, but in New York's Museum of Modern Art.

193. 'West Side,' a Chair by Ettore Sottsass, c1980

This striking chair is by Ettore Sottsass who was one of the organizers of the radical Memphis Collection, an exhibition of 1981. He has been described as a metaphoric designer, the object itself being of little importance, but the conflict between colour, shape and structure is exploited to amuse and upset the eye. Sottsass was born in Austria in 1917, has worked extensively in Italy as consultant designer to Olivetti, and also studied at the Royal College of Art.

191

193

192

Monarchs

The names of English and French monarchs are often used to denote the period of a piece of furniture when the precise date of manufacture is not known.

In some cases a ruler is closely associated with a recognisable style; Louis XIV, for instance, saw the development of the decorative arts in France as a matter of policy and the massive formal designs of his time reflect the elaboration of life at his court. Dramatic upheavals such as the French Revolution brought about dramatic changes in style but generally changes of style were gradual and overlapped the reigns of different monarchs.

In Britain especially, the machinery of fashion tended to be more loosely linked to the sovereign and public taste was influenced by a variety of factors. This was especially true during the reign of long-lived monarchs like George III (1760-1820) and the names of the producers of cabinetmakers' pattern books, like Chippendale, Sheraton and Hepplewhite are often used quite freely to denote the style of their times. These cabinetmakers were influential not necessarily because of their designs but because they recorded contemporary styles, some of which of course may have been their own.

American furniture periods tend to be classified using a mixture of English monarchs and makers, and the dating is complicated by the fact that it took a long time for European styles to cross the Atlantic so that the American period occurs several years behind the corresponding period in Britain. For example, Queen Anne died in 1714, but the American Queen Anne style is taken to cover the period 1720-1750.

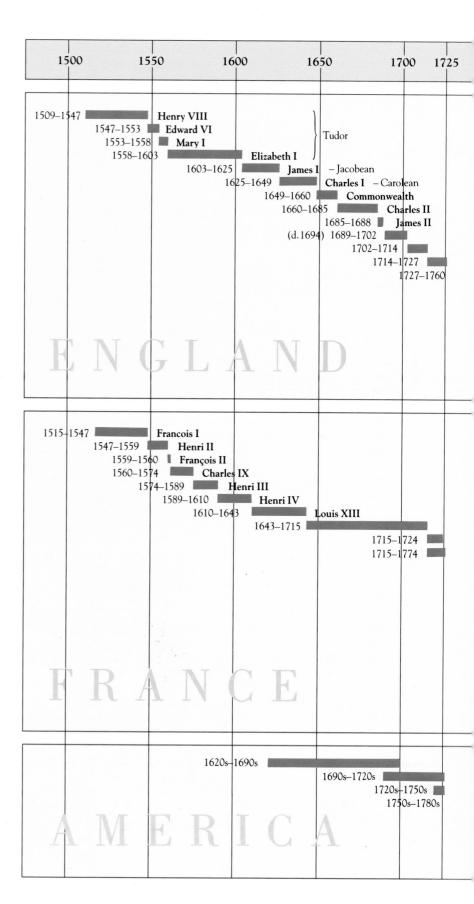

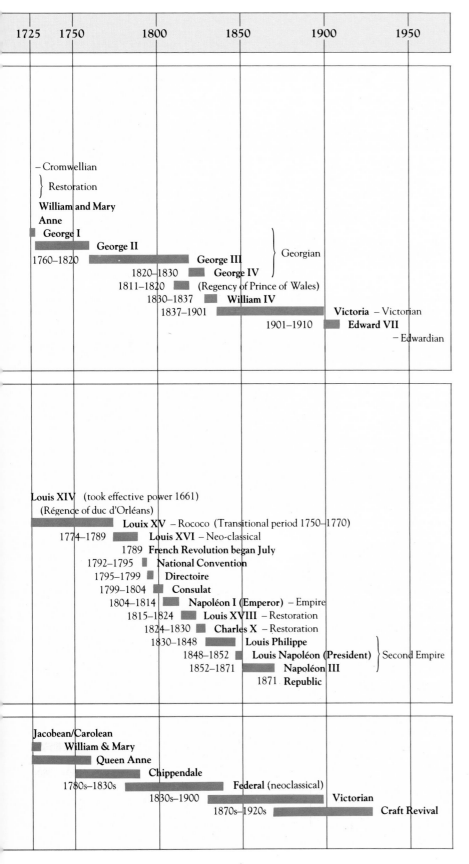

| 1725 | 1750 | 1800 | 1850 | 1900 | 1950 |

– Cromwellian
} Restoration
William and Mary
Anne
George I
1760–1820 **George II**
George III } Georgian
1820–1830 **George IV**
1811–1820 (Regency of Prince of Wales)
1830–1837 **William IV**
1837–1901 **Victoria** – Victorian
1901–1910 **Edward VII**
– Edwardian

Louis XIV (took effective power 1661)
(Régence of duc d'Orléans)
Louix XV – Rococo (Transitional period 1750–1770)
1774–1789 **Louis XVI** – Neo-classical
1789 **French Revolution began July**
1792–1795 **National Convention**
1795–1799 **Directoire**
1799–1804 **Consulat**
1804–1814 **Napoléon I (Emperor)** – Empire
1815–1824 **Louis XVIII** – Restoration
1824–1830 **Charles X** – Restoration
1830–1848 **Louis Philippe**
1848–1852 **Louis Napoléon (President)** } Second Empire
1852–1871 **Napoléon III**
1871 **Republic**

Jacobean/Carolean
William & Mary
Queen Anne
Chippendale
1780s–1830s **Federal** (neoclassical)
1830s–1900 **Victorian**
1870s–1920s **Craft Revival**

Cabinetmakers' pattern books and other influential publications

Listed here is a selection of books influential both on the furniture makers and designers of their times and on furniture historians.

Stalker and Parker, **Treatise of Japanning and Varnishing**, 1688

Thomas Chippendale, **Gentleman and Cabinet-Maker's Director**, 1754 (2nd edition 1755; 3rd edition 1762)

Ince and Mayhew, **Universal System of Household Furniture**, 1759–1762

Robert Manwaring, **Cabinet and Chair-Maker's Real Friend and Companion** 1765

Robert and James Adam, **Works in Architecture**, 1773–1778 (2nd volume 1779; 3rd volume 1822)

George Hepplewhite, **Cabinet-Maker and Upholsterer's Guide**, 1788

Thomas Shearer, Hepplewhite and others, **Cabinet-Maker's London Book of Prices**, 1788

Thomas Sheraton, **Cabinet-Maker and Upholsterer's Drawing-Book**, 1791–1794

Percier and Fontaine, **Receuil des décorations intérieurs**, 1801 (2nd edition 1812)

Thomas Sheraton, **Cabinet Dictionary**, 1803

Thomas Hope, **Household Furniture and Interior Decoration**, 1807

George Smith, **Collection of Designs for Household Furniture and Interior Decoration**, 1808

Collection of Ornamental Designs after the Antique, 1812

Cabinet Maker and Upholsterer's Guide, 1826

John C. Loudon, **Encyclopaedia of Cottage, Farm and Villa Furniture**, 1833
Augustus W.N. Pugin, **Gothic Furniture in the style of the 15th century**, 1835

The True Principle of Pointed or Christian Architecture, 1841

Bruce Talbert, **Gothic Forms Applied to Furniture**, 1867

Charles Eastlake, **Hints on Household Taste**, 1868

121

acanthus – A classical ornamental device based on the prickly, indented leaves of the acanthus plant, used especially in the capitals of Corinthian and Composite columns.

anthemion – A classical ornament consisting of a band of alternating floral forms based on the honeysuckle flower. A single motif based on the honeysuckle is also called an anthemion.

apron – An ornamental projection below a rail, often shaped and carved.

arcading – A series of round-topped arches, frequently used decoratively, especially on early carved furniture.

astragal – A small half-round moulding frequently used for glazing bars.

ball and claw foot – A foot in the form of a claw clutching a ball, often used in conjunction with a cabriole leg and popular in England and America in the 18th century.

baluster (banister) – A short supporting column, bulbous near the base, used in series to form a balustrade.

baluster back – A chair with a splat of baluster outline.

baluster–turned – See turned leg.

balustrade – See baluster.

banding – Veneer was often used in bands to form decorative borders to the main surface. Crossbanding was cut across the grain, while feather or herringbone banding was cut with the grain at an angle so that two strips laid side by side resembled a feather.

banister – See baluster.

barleysugar-turned – See turned leg.

baroque – A decorative style which originated in Italy and reached its height in the 17th century, characterised by heavy and exuberant forms. Its influence varied from country to country but baroque furniture tends to be sculptural and often architectural in form and is frequently gilded, with human figures, scrolls and shells much in evidence.

beading – A three-dimensional decorative motif in the form of a series of round beads in a single line or a very fine half-round moulding (see cock beading).

Biedermeier – A German term used to denote both the period 1815–1848 and the decorative style popular in Germany, Austria and Scandinavia from the 1820s to the 1840s, which was characterised by solid, unpretentious furniture in light-coloured woods. Biedermeier was a newspaper caricature symbolising the uncultured bourgeoisie.

bobbin-turned – See turned leg.

bombé – An exaggerated curved and swollen form characteristic of the rococo style.

brown furniture – A term used by the antiques trade to refer to the plain English mahogany furniture of the Georgian period.

bulb-turned – See turned leg.

burl – The American term for burr.

burr – See veneer.

C-scroll – A scroll in the shape of a letter C, a favourite rococo motif.

cabochon – An oval or round boss used decoratively, usually in conjunction with other motifs.

cabriole leg – A sinuous tapering leg, curving outwards at the knee, in towards the ankle and out again at the foot.

canted – When legs or projected members are set at an angle to the corner of a piece they are known as canted legs or canted corners.

capital – The head of a column, usually decorated according to the different architectural orders, i.e. Doric (plain disc-like capital), Ionic (with four scroll corners), Corinthian (decorated with bands of acanthus leaves), Composite (a combination of Ionic and Corinthian).

cartouche – An ornamental panel, often a stylised shield, which is decorative itself but can also carry an inscription, a monogram or a crest.

caryatid – An architectural motif consisting of a column in the form of a male or female figure which is also often found on carved furniture and as a bronze mount.

castors – Small swivelling wheels attached to the bottom of furniture, to make it easier to move the piece.

chamfer – A narrow flat surface formed by cutting away the apex of an angle between two surfaces, thus removing the sharp edge. Hence chamfered leg, chamfered stretcher etc.

chasing – The tooling of a metal's surface. Bronze furniture mounts were chased after casting to remove blemishes and sharpen the detail before gilding.

chinoiserie – A Western imitation of Chinese decoration, usually more fanciful than accurate and frequently used to give an exotic touch to a basically European design.

ciseleur – French for craftsman who used a variety of chisels and other tools to finish bronze mounts once they had been cast by a *fondeur* or founder. After finishing they were usually gilded by a *doreur*. Under the 18th century Paris guild system the *fondeurs-ciseleurs* and the *doreurs* had separate Corporations.

cornucopia – A horn of plenty, used decoratively as a shell-like horn overflowing with fruit.

cresting – The carved ornament on the top rail of a chair-back.

cresting rail – See top rail.

crocket – A leaf-like projection frequently placed on angles, arches and pinnacles in gothic architecture and found as a decorative device on gothic style furniture.

crossbanding – See banding.

cut-card work – A form of slightly raised decoration mainly used on silverware, consisting of thin sheets cut into patterns and soldered onto the surface.

doreur – See ciseleur.

drop-in seat – A removable upholstered or caned seat which rests on blocks inside the seat rails of a chair.

ébéniste – A French term for a cabinetmaker, a specialist in veneered furniture, as distinct from a *menuisier* or joiner who specialised in carved pieces like chairs or beds. A *maître* of the Paris furniture makers' guild (*Corporation des menuisiers-ébénistes*) was not bound to specialise, but the distinction was generally observed until the end of the 18th century.

estampille – The stamp with the name and initials of a *maître ébéniste* which was obligatory on French furniture from about 1750 until the Revolution. The mark was struck with a cold punch rather than branded, although delicate pieces could be signed in ink. Long names were sometimes shortened, as

in BVRB for Bernard van Risenburgh, and the marks were usually in an inconspicuous place, often accompanied by the monogram of the *Corporation des Jurés Menuisiers-Ébénistes* – JME conjoined – a quality control mark. Furniture made for the crown did not have to be stamped and royal craftsmen were exempt.

festoon – A neo-classical decorative motif in the form of a looped garland of flowers, fruit and foliage.

figure – The natural grain patterns of a veneer are known as figuring.

finial – An ornamental projection from the top of a piece of furniture, often a knob, ball, acorn, urn or flame.

fluting – Decorative in the form of shallow, parallel grooves, especially on columns and pilasters or on the legs of furniture.

fondeur – See ciseleur.

fretwork – Carved geometrical patterns, either in relief or pierced, or sawn with a fretsaw.

gadroon – A form of decorative edging usually in the form of a series of convex curved lobes or repeated spiral ribs resembling ropetwist.

gilding – The application of gold to the surface of another material. Bronze mounts were frequently gilded to prevent tarnishing, especially in France. Wood was also gilded for decorative effect.

gilt – See gilding.

Gothic – A decorative style based on the pointed arches, cluster columns, spires and other elements of late medieval architecture. Gothic revivals have influenced furniture design at several periods, particularly in Britain in the mid-18th century and again in the mid-19th century.

grisaille – Monochrome decoration in tones of grey.

inlay – Although it is often used to mean marquetry, inlay strictly refers to decorative materials like ivory or ebony set into the surface of solid wood, unlike veneer which covers the whole surface.

japanning – The term used in America and Britain for techniques imitating the Oriental lacquerwork which began to arrive in Europe via the Dutch East India Company in the 17th century.

joinery – Joined furniture is formed of vertical and horizontal members, united by mortice and tenon joints and supporting panels.

joint (joyned, joined) stool – A contemporary term for the mortice and tenon jointed stools of the 16th and 17th centuries, used now to refer specifically to stools with four turned legs, joined by stretchers near the feet and rails just below a rectangular seat.

maître – A mastercraftsman under the Paris guild system, who was entitled to own a workshop and stamp his pieces, having served an apprenticeship and paid the necessary fees. See *estampille*.

marchand-mercier – Under the Paris guild system marchands- merciers combined the roles of furniture dealers and interior decorators. They were not allowed to run their own workshops but often exerted considerable influence on fashion by acting as intermediaries between customer and craftsman.

marquetry – The use of veneers (woods of different colours, bone, ivory, mother-of-pearl, tortoiseshell, etc.) to form decorative designs like scrolls, flowers and landscapes. Abstract geometrical patterns formed in the same manner are known as parquetry.

member – Any of the structural components (rails, uprights, stretchers etc.) of a piece of joined furniture.

menuisier – See *ébéniste*.

mortice and tenon joint – The basic method of joining the framework of a piece of furniture. The tenon is a projection (usually a slim rectangle) at the end of a rail which fits exactly into the mortice, a cavity cut in the side of an upright. The tenon is normally secured by dowels.

moulding – A length of wood or other material applied to the surface of a piece of furniture. The shaped section of a moulding is usually made up from a number of curves, and there are various standard types (astragal, ogee, cavetto, ovolo) mostly of architectural origin.

mounts – Decorative motifs, usually of brass or gilt-bronze, fixed to cabinetwork.

neo-classicism – The predominant decorative style of the second half of the 18th century. Based on the restrained use of Greek and Roman architectural form and ornament, it is characterised by a sober, rectilinear emphasis which was a conscious reaction to the exuberance of the rococo.

ormolu – Gilt bronze. A term derived from the French *or moulu* (literally ground gold).

panel – A flat surface supported by rails and stiles in joined furniture.

parcel gilt – Gilded in part only.

parquetry – See marquetry.

patera – A neo-classical decorative motif, either oval or round, resembling a stylised flower or rosette.

pierced – Carved ornament is described as pierced when the decoration is cut right through the piece, as in fretwork.

pilaster – A shallow column attached to a piece of furniture.

putto (pl. putti) – A naked infant, often winged, used as a decorative motif. Also referred to as a cherub, a cupid or an amoretto.

rail – A horizontal member used in the construction of joined furniture.

reeding – Decoration in the form of parallel ribbing, especially on columns and pilasters or on the legs of furniture.

Renaissance – The rebirth of ancient Roman values in the arts which began in Italy in the 14th century and gradually replaced the gothic style in most of Europe during the following two and a half centuries. Renaissance designers were inspired by the sculpture and architectural remains of the ancient world and their furniture reflects this in the profusion of carved ornament.

repoussé work – A form of embossed decoration produced by hammering sheet metal from the underside.

rocaille – Stylised and fanciful rock and shell decoration, used by extension to refer to many of the decorative forms of the rococo.

rococo – A decorative style which spread from France during the first half of the 18th century, characterised by delicate curved outlines, C-

scrolls, fantastic organic forms and a tendency towards asymmetry in ornamental details.

sabre leg – A furniture leg which is curved and tapered like a cavalry sabre.

seat rail – The horizontal framework which supports the seat of a joined chair.

serpentine – In the form of an undulating curve, convex at the centre and concave on each side.

spindle – A slim, turned rod frequently used as an upright in chair backs.

splat – The central upright member of a chair back which joins the seat to the top rail.

square-section leg – A leg which would be square if cut at right-angles, but which may also be tapering or shaped in some other way.

stile – A vertical member used in the construction of joined furniture.

strapwork – A form of decoration particularly popular in Northern Europe in the 16th and 17th centuries, resembling interlaced, pierced and scrolled bands of leather.

stretcher – A horizontal crosspiece used to join and strengthen the legs of a piece of furniture.

stringing – Thin strips of wood or metal inlay used to decorate furniture.

strung border – A border decorated with stringing.

stuff-over – A term used when the upholstery of a chair covers the framework rather than being a panel within it. Hence stuff-over seat.

swag – A decorative motif in the form of a loop of cloth and similar to a festoon.

thrown chair – An alternative name for a turned chair (qv), derived from throwing, an old term for turning.

timbers – Another name for the heavy wooden framework of a piece of furniture.

top rail – The topmost horizontal member which joins the uprights of a chair back. Also known as a yoke rail or a cresting rail.

turned chair – A chair made up entirely of turned uprights and rails, often incorporating large numbers of decoratively turned spindles. A form popular in the 16th and 17th centuries, often with three legs and triangular seats.

turned leg – A leg shaped on a lathe, usually circular in section and mainly fashionable before the beginning of the 18th century. Turned legs are found in many traditional patterns, e.g. bobbin – a series of small bulbs or bobbins; bobbin and ring – small bulbs interspaced by rings; bulb – a large bulbous swelling of elongated melon form, often carved and used with a base and capital to form a leg; barley-sugar or barley-twist – a double spiral resembling a barleysugar sweet; vase – in the shape of a vase, usually slim at the base and gradually increasing in diameter towards the top; baluster – in the shape of a baluster, bulbous at the base and slim towards the top.

under-frame – The supporting structure of a piece of furniture, including legs, stretchers and any other braces.

uprights – The vertical parts of a chair back, formed as continuations of the rear legs.

vase-turned – See turned leg.

veneer – A very thin sheet, usually of wood, applied to the surface of a piece of furniture. Veneers cut from knotty areas of the tree are particularly decorative and known as burrs, hence burr walnut.

vernis martin – A generic term for all varnish and lacquer (japanning) used in France in imitation of oriental lacquer, but specifically referring to the four Martin brothers, who were granted a monopoly on imitation relief lacquer in 1730, which was renewed in 1744.

vitruvian scroll – A classically-derived ornamental device in the form of a series of scrolls resembling waves.

x-frame – An arrangement of diagonal stretchers joining the front and back legs of a piece of furniture and crossing to form an X.

x-stretcher – See x-frame.

yoke rail – See top rail.

These drawings taken from Chippendale's *The Gentleman & Cabinetmaker's Director* are not for one-armed chairs, but are designs for suites of chairs showing how an armchair and a dining chair might look; likewise the legs are different, giving alternatives to the carver and the client.

These are very rococo chairs: all the rails are carved with rocaille, foliage, scrolls and other frippery. The cabriole legs are interesting, showing an English version with a paw foot and a dolphin as a concession to French taste.

Just as Chippendale had no hesitation bringing in elements of French designs, he combined the result with European-made 'Chinese' fabric which was very popular in the mid-18th century. The frames would almost certainly have been gilded, unlike Chinese chairs.

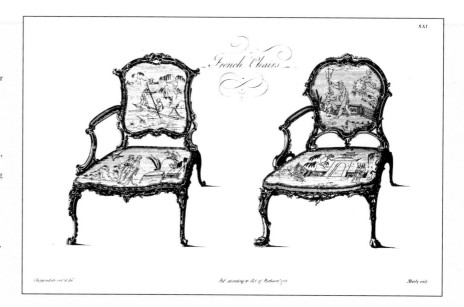

NINETEENTH CENTURY SWIVEL CHAIR WITH SPRING MECHANISM

FROM THE GREAT EXHIBITION AT CRYSTAL PALACE IN 1851

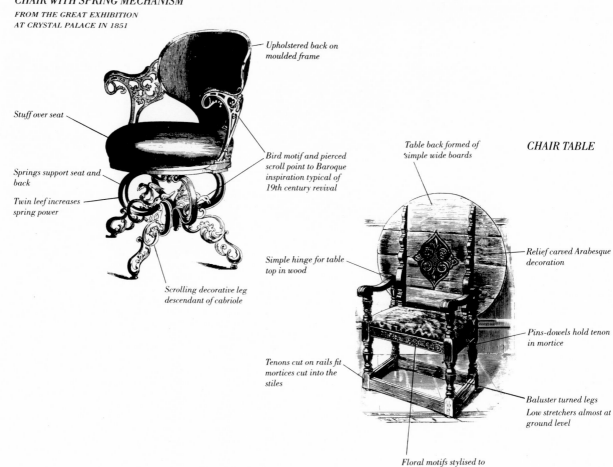

Upholstered back on moulded frame

Stuff over seat

Springs support seat and back

Twin leef increases spring power

Bird motif and pierced scroll point to Baroque inspiration typical of 19th century revival

Scrolling decorative leg descendant of cabriole

Table back formed of simple wide boards

CHAIR TABLE

Relief carved Arabesque decoration

Simple hinge for table top in wood

Pins-dowels hold tenon in mortice

Tenons cut on rails fit mortices cut into the stiles

Baluster turned legs
Low stretchers almost at ground level

Floral motifs stylised to decorate the frieze

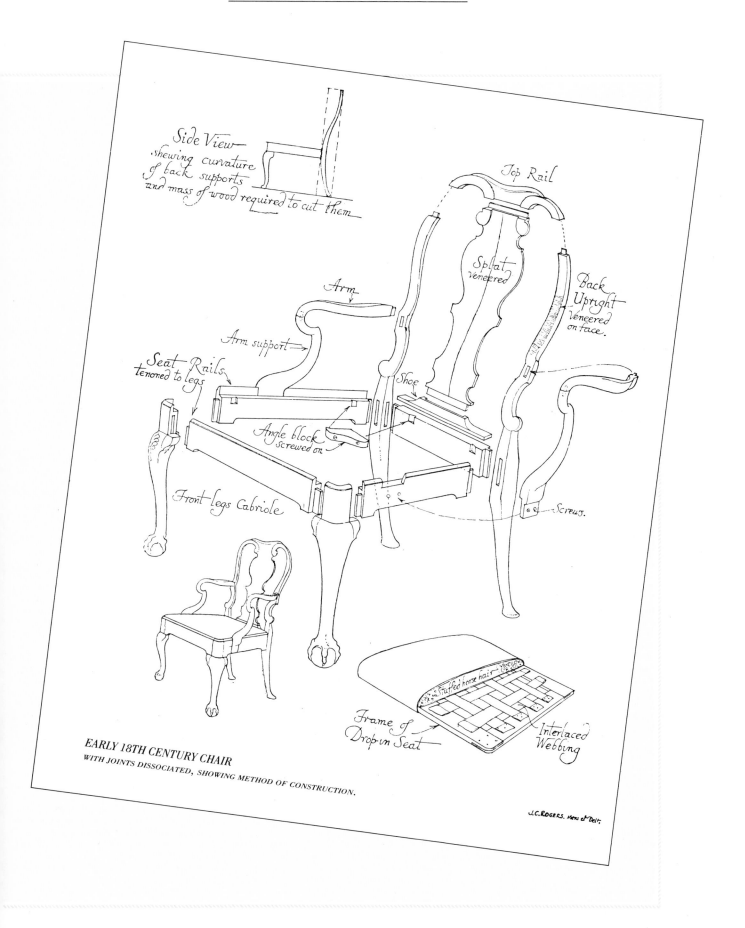

Side View
shewing curvature
of back supports
and mass of wood required to cut them

Top Rail

Arm

Splat
veneered

Back
Upright
veneered
on face.

Arm support

Seat Rails
tenoned to legs

Shoe

Angle block
screwed on

Front legs Cabriole

Screws.

Frame of
Drop-in Seat

Stuffed horse hair

Interlaced
Webbing

EARLY 18TH CENTURY CHAIR
WITH JOINTS DISSOCIATED, SHOWING METHOD OF CONSTRUCTION.

J.C.ROGERS. Mens et Delt.